The Seventh TRUMPET & the Seven THUNDERS

Read many more Stendal books, available from
www.lifesentencepublishing.com, and wherever books are sold

The Seventh
TRUMPET
& the Seven
THUNDERS

God's Prophetic Plan Revealed

Russell M. Stendal

LIFE SENTENCE
Publishing, LLC

Watch Russell's video introduction:

www.lifesentencepublishing.com

Like us on Facebook

The Seventh Trumpet and the Seven Thunders – Russell M. Stendal

Copyright © 2013

PRINTED IN THE UNITED STATES OF AMERICA

First edition published 2013

LIFE SENTENCE Publishing books are available at discounted prices for ministries and other outreach. Find out more by contacting info@lifesentencepublishing.com

LIFE SENTENCE Publishing and its logo are trademarks of

LIFE SENTENCE Publishing, LLC
P.O. BOX 652
Abbotsford, WI 54405

Paperback ISBN: 978-1-62245-098-5

Ebook ISBN: 978-1-62245-099-2

10 9 8 7 6 5 4 3 2 1

This book is available from www.lifesentencepublishing.com, www.amazon.com, Barnes & Noble, and your local Christian bookstore

Cover Designer: Amber Burger

Editor: Sheila Wilkinson

Contents

CHAPTER 1

The Prophecy of Noah's Ark

W e interpret much of the Old Testament in light of the New Testament, but the keys to the signs and symbols of the book of The Revelation of Jesus Christ are found in the Old Testament. This is where we discover the message of the seventh trumpet. It will sound along with the previous six trumpets on the last day, but the Lord has been sounding this message throughout all of history. The trumpet symbolizes the direct voice of God and the gospel of redemption. It was blown to warn of danger and announce that there is shelter and protection in God. God helps us see the end from the beginning.

Genesis is the book of beginnings, but it also tells us what is going to happen at the end. The Lord knows from the beginning what will be the end of the matter. Our ancestors lost the blessing of God almost from the beginning. Yet the Lord has offered His plan of salvation both to us and to them. Some will be inside His plan of salvation, and others will remain outside. But Scripture is very clear: It says that the Lord is not willing that any should perish (2 Peter 3:9). He wants to give everyone an opportunity. We have already seen that the Lord gave another opportunity to Cain even after he killed his brother Abel. God did not immediately decree the sentence that Cain deserved. He said that Cain could continue to live on the earth but that he would wander and never be at rest (Genesis 4:12).

What did Cain do? He tried to do the opposite of this; he established a city. But the line of Cain came to a violent end. His line went from bad to worse. God said that if anyone were to kill Cain he would be avenged seven times. The great-great-great grandson of Cain (who curiously was named Lamech, which means "overthrower") said that if Cain shall be avenged sevenfold, truly Lamech seventy times seven (Genesis 4:24).

In Colombia, we have seen how one innocent or unjust death can generate many more deaths, because people are looking for those responsible and then make mistakes by killing the wrong people. One death can degenerate into an out-of-control chain of events. And how great a curse has been generated after so many innocent deaths that we have seen. God said the curse would affect the earth, and the earth would no longer give forth her strength. So problems began at the very roots of how society was to be sustained. Contrast this with the Lord Jesus who told Peter that he should forgive not seven times but until seventy times seven (Matthew 18:22).

In regard to spiritual things, we are like ground that can be good or bad, under a curse or under a blessing. If all the land is full of the curse and corruption, what will happen? Look at what happened in Genesis 6. After having eliminated an entire generation (that of Abel), we have the generation of Cain that ends with Lamech. There is also the generation of Adam, much of which ended with another Lamech who was the father of Noah and who lived 777 years. Noah's grandfather Methuselah lived 969 years. Methuselah means "when he dies, it shall come." What shall come? God was going to wipe out everyone with the exception of one family. This is how it goes:

Genesis 6

1. *And it came to pass, when men began to multiply on the face of the earth and daughters were born unto them,*

2. that the sons of God saw that the daughters of men were fair, and they took for themselves wives of all whom they chose.

Much controversy exists over this, because strange doctrines have come forth saying that the "sons of God" were angels, and the "daughters of men" were humans, and that this caused mixed offspring like the mythology of the Greek gods. I do not believe this is what happened here. What I understand is that from the beginning, in the creation (and ratified by Jesus in the gospel), He created one man for one woman. He said that from the beginning this was so (Matthew 19:4, 8). Man has always felt the need for a helpmeet. God brought Eve forth out of Adam and brought her to him. And in the plan of God throughout the Scripture, when there is a true man of God, God provides the woman for this person. In the case of Isaac, they sent for Rebecca. God was in that matter and many more.

> *What I understand is that from the beginning, in the creation (and ratified by Jesus in the gospel), He created one man for one woman.*

The Lord Jesus will return one day for a clean bride without spot or wrinkle or any such thing. Jesus doesn't pretend to know when this is, because it is His Father, God the Father, who is preparing the bride by the Holy Spirit (this is a bride of many members encompassing all the true people of God). So what was the problem before the flood? The sons of God started choosing whatever woman looked good to them, and they caused a huge problem because they did not leave the knowledge of good and evil in the hands of God. We know that many people throughout history have accepted that when God has given us commandments, when God tells us not to do something, we should obey. But the problem with the human race is that they have never wanted to cede the knowledge of good back to God. And this is what happened here. They wanted to choose women – as many as they wanted. And look what the Lord said after all of this:

> 3. *And the LORD said, My spirit shall not always strive with man, for certainly he is flesh; yet his days shall be one hundred and twenty years.*

This is the first time God puts a limit on the days of man, but it is after the flood that we really notice the effect. The long lives of the patriarchs began to diminish. This number of 120 is very interesting also, because 120 is the number that signifies the maximum that God will allow man to live without God. God said, *My spirit shall not always strive with man,* and then it's as if He says, "I see that this is very serious. I am going to limit the time that man has here, and he will age sooner." But curiously, the word *hope* occurs in exactly 120 verses throughout the Bible. What is the hope of the Gentiles? It is a new covenant in which God wants to change our hearts. He wants to put His life in our hearts because our own life, when we do what we think is good, causes trouble in very short order.

As I have said before, we allow things to happen in our own lives and justify them, but we condemn these same actions in the lives of others. If we begin to embrace something for ourselves and give free rein to our ego, our greed, etc., we justify this as long as it pertains to us. But when someone else does it, we condemn them for doing the exact same thing. This is the life of the natural man. Then it says:

> 4. *There were giants in the earth in those days,* [There were some guys who wanted to have everything] *and also after that, when the sons of God came in unto the daughters of men.*

From the beginning, there was the idea that some are born free and others are born slaves. From the beginning, God told Eve that she would be called woman because she was taken out of man. If the man was free, then the woman was also free, but they did not stay free for very long. After they took the knowledge of good and evil for themselves, they were sent away from the presence of God and ended up as slaves. The only way back into true liberty is what the New Testament calls being born again by the Spirit of God, by the life of God, because Jesus came that we might have life and have it more abundantly (John 10:10). It also says that *where that Spirit of the Lord is, there is liberty* (2 Corinthians 3:17). There is no liberty where the Spirit of the Lord is absent.

Therefore, those men of old, seeking freedom, seeking what they had lost, began to take whatever woman seemed fair in their eyes and kept her. The next step was to subjugate others by force. So they were the giants. They were the big guys. They dominated. Then they modified human vocabulary along with the evolution of human history, so they became the nobility, and everyone else was common or vulgar (born slaves). Nobility is born that way because people have power and dominion and everyone else is born their slaves. Note that the evolution of man went from being free sons of God to becoming "beasts," moved only by slavery to carnal, sensual, corrupt desires, in slavery to one another and, of course, in slavery to the devil.

What happens today is slightly different in that we do not have slave markets where people in chains of iron or brass are bought and sold. Today we have credit cards and work contracts, and people have to sign documents down at the bank where they are charged interest. Modern slavery takes a different form.

But there are others who think that they belong to modern day "nobility." They believe that it is their destiny to control the lives of everyone else for one reason or another, because they were born into a family of power or money. Here are the roots to this:

Genesis 6

5. And GOD saw that the wickedness of man was great in the earth and that every imagination of the thoughts of his heart was only evil continually.

When man desired to control the knowledge of good and of evil, he did not even end up doing good most of the time. God says that ALL the time, always, man's desires and intent were evil.

6. And the LORD repented of having made man on the earth, and it grieved him at his heart.

Remember that we were created in the likeness and image of God; the emotions that God feels are something that we are also designed to feel. God has the sovereignty, but we also have a will that is capable of making decisions. And God was grieved in His heart. He knew what could happen when He gave man free will. When the Scripture mentions *the Lamb that was slain from the foundation of the world* (Revelation 13:8), it indicates that the Lord Jesus and His Father were willing in advance to implement a plan of redemption in case the free will of man took things in the wrong direction. And it did not take very long. All the indirect evidence seems to indicate that they only lasted about twelve years in paradise – a very short time. It grieved the Lord in His heart.

7. And the LORD said, I will destroy man whom I have created from the face of the earth, both man and beast and the animals and the fowls of the air; for I repent of having made them.

God did not say, "Let's allow this to go on a bit more and we will see what happens." God came to the conclusion that what the natural man was doing ALL the time was evil in the eyes of God. Everything! There was nothing good being done by man on the face of the earth. What was man doing? He was taking women who seemed "fair" and subjecting the rest of humanity by brute force. Yet here in verse 8 is something that changes the picture:

8. *But Noah found grace in the eyes of the LORD.*

This is the first use of the word *grace* in the Scriptures. And the word *grace* is one of the most important words in the vocabulary of God. We have been taught that grace is supposed to mean unmerited favor, and in a certain sense it does, but this is not the principal definition of the word *grace*. The most important part of

> *And the word grace is one of the most important words in the vocabulary of God.*

the word *grace* has to do with the power of God to intervene, to save us, and even to correct us as necessary. It is when God intervenes to do for us what we are unable to do for ourselves. But He will also involve us. Some people claim that we are saved by grace and that works do not matter. Well, in the ancient time leading up to Noah, the works of all humanity, even what they thought was good, the Lord says was really evil. The apostle James in his letter says that *faith without works is dead*. And in the epistle to the Ephesians, it says that *by grace are ye saved through faith*. So notice how this works. Here is a prime example from the beginning of the history of God's plan for salvation:

8. *But Noah found grace in the eyes of the LORD.*

9. *These are the generations of Noah. Noah was a just man and perfect in his generations, and Noah walked with God.*

10. *And Noah begat three sons, Shem, Ham, and Japheth.*

To be perfect is as simple as walking with God. It is for sure that God directed Noah. God provided a wife for Noah. God was with the family of Noah. Scripture says he was perfect in his generations. His generations were three sons who would each have descendants, and each son also had a wife. And they were all saved by grace when the ancient world was destroyed. But see that it went quite a bit further than just a mental belief that they had the grace of God.

They had to work for close to a hundred years building an ark, and the ark had to be made exactly according to the plan of God. If the ark had been defective and failed, even being in the ark would not have done them any good. The ark had to be well built. God gave the plans. God did a lot of things. He sent the animals, and Scripture says He even sealed the door. But Noah, his wife, their three sons, and their three daughters-in-law did the work. And it was work that was directed and approved by God.

All this took place when God said that what the rest of humanity was doing was so evil that He could not put up with it any longer. It was not that they were a little bit off. They were so off track that God decided to destroy them from the face of the earth. How are we doing in Colombia? How are the works of the people of Colombia? How about in the United States? Or in any other country? What is God thinking about all this? Does He think that we are doing *evil continually*?

The good ideas of humanity turn out to be not so good from God's point of view. This is why He did not accept Cain's present.

The produce that Cain worked so hard for and offered to the Lord, the Lord did not receive. On the other hand, his brother Abel cared for his sheep and sacrificed one and presented it to the Lord and the Lord approved. Why? Because the work of our hands, if not linked to a blood covenant, is unacceptable. The blood covenant means we know that, in and of our own life, we cannot ever please God. Our thoughts, our works, and all that we think is good, is not good according to Him. The only thing good is if we come and rest in the life of Christ who is the real Lamb of God. Then He can change our hearts, He can change our desires, and He can change our thoughts. We can begin to want what God wants, and we can be moved by God, starting with our conscience. This was the difference between Cain and Abel. Those who are true to God have struggled against those who work according to the ways of this world ever since the beginning.

This world began with lies, death, and a curse. The entire ancient world was caught up in this except for Noah, because Noah found grace. And the fact that Noah found grace resulted in a different family where God ordered the family and where the sons of Noah did not wind up with just any girl that appeared on the scene. Their wives were provided by the Lord. This is why God said that Noah was perfect in his generations. How was Noah singled out for this grace? His name means "rest." Maybe Noah just quit doing what everyone else was doing and waited for the Lord to lead him and guide him. Maybe he just decided to cease and desist and began to cry out to God for help.

11. *The earth corrupted itself before God, and the earth filled itself with violence.*

What is violence? In old terminology, there is a word for *power,* a word for *power under control*, and a word for *violence*. Power is what many seek. Jesus had (and has) access to all power, but when on earth, He never did His own will, only the will of His Father who sent Him. If we are sons of God, the Lord wants to give us gifts of the Spirit of God, gifts of power. But many go off the rails with these gifts. The Lord is watching to see who will use these gifts according to His control. Violence is power out of control. Violence is when those of this world take the law into their own hands and begin to implement justice their own way. This never ends well (even with Hollywood movies to the contrary).

> 12. *And God looked upon the earth, and, behold, it was corrupt, for all flesh had corrupted its way upon the earth.*

> 13. *And God said unto Noah, The end of all flesh is come before me, for the earth is filled with violence through them; and, behold, I will destroy them with the earth.*

> 14. *Make thee an ark of cedar trees; rooms shalt thou make in the ark and shalt reconcile it within and without covering it over with pitch* [Hebrew "ransom" or "atonement"].

Note that the translation is a bit different. This is the first usage of the word *reconcile* in its various forms, which is used in 140 verses in Scripture. One of the last uses is when Paul, in one of his epistles, said that God has given us *the ministry of reconciliation*. It is important to know what reconciliation is. In this first usage of the term in the Bible, Noah is ordered to seal the ark. This is not the word for *pitch* that is used elsewhere in Scripture, and the last word in verse 14 is the first usage of the Hebrew word that is translated "ransom" or "atonement" in the rest of the Bible. This refers to the blood, because the

Lord Jesus gave His life for us; He gave His blood as a ransom or atonement for us.

And Noah's ark is a symbol of God's plan of salvation. It had rooms and three levels. In God's plan of salvation, there are three feasts. First is the Feast of the Passover, where the blood is applied, where there is teaching regarding the law of God, and where anyone can come and offer their sacrifice. (Jesus was the sacrifice for us to kill the power of sin forever and to kill the guilt, so we might be once again justified before God and be presented as living sacrifices, clean peace offerings before the Lord.) Holiness is being separated for the exclusive use of the Lord, and this is what the Passover is all about.

...they were seeking to use God that they might be blessed and prosper in their old nature with their insatiable desires for all that they saw in the world...

People have distorted this, and what is now done in Holy Week celebrations when many people think they are doing good is similar to what was going on in the ancient world before the flood. Everything was evil in God's eyes, even what they thought was good! Why? Because they were seeking to use God that they might be blessed and prosper in their old nature with their insatiable desires for all that they saw in the world around them, starting with beautiful women.

The second level of the ark is the Feast of Pentecost where the Lord sends His Spirit to give not the fullness of the inheritance in Christ, but the earnest (down payment) to those who have truly been born again into the priesthood of all believers in the body of Christ (Ephesians 1:14).

The third level is the Feast of Tabernacles. "Tabernacles" is God dwelling with and in His corporate people. This is what the Lord wants. But He cannot fully dwell in us – and we cannot fully dwell with Him – if we continue with our insatiable desires and if we continue to insist on preferring the knowledge of good and evil instead of the tree of life. He is the tree of life, and if we really want to be with Him, it will cost us the other.

In the Song of Solomon, the Shulamite, who is a symbol of the real bride of the Lord Jesus, wakes up under an apple tree in the arms of her lover (Jesus) (see Song of Solomon 8:5). Where was it that the human race fell asleep, dead in trespasses and sin? They died under an apple tree, under the wrong tree, because they did not pick the tree of life (Him).

> 14. *Make thee an ark of cedar trees; rooms shalt thou make in the ark and shalt reconcile it within and without with pitch* [Hebrew "ransom" or "atonement"].

How is this reconciliation? Shipwrights still use this term. They must reconcile each plank to the keel, which has to go straight through the center of the ship. And if the planks do not line up straight, they will not seal. Reconciliation is defined here in its first use in Scripture and throughout the rest of its trajectory through the Bible into the New Testament. Reconciliation according to God is not to just meet God halfway. It is not for us to give up the "mortal" sins and keep the "venial" sins. This is not reconciliation with God. People even seal it with a "sacrament" of reconciliation. Many evangelicals do it another way. But the true reconciliation with God is to be holy as He is holy, to be righteous as He is righteous, and to be perfect as He is perfect. Noah was perfect and righteous in all his generations. If we read on a little further, we come to a part where Noah does not seem to have been so perfect.

David was a man after God's own heart, with a perfect heart before God. But if we read all about the life of David, there are some things that do not seem to be so perfect. If we continue to read God's book, sometimes what was wrong is not in there

(David's sin does not appear in the book of Chronicles). When God forgives, when He restores, and when He cleanses, we can be made clean. When God forgives, He forgets.

This is no longer about us but about the Lord Jesus who gave His life for us. We are hopeless sinners, but He is not, and He wants to reign and rule from the throne of our hearts until we are clean (and if we continue to accept His authority, He can keep us clean; see 1 John 1:9). Noah's ark was reconciled within and without. Jesus covers us in the same way. He covers us within and without until He finishes His work in us – all by the grace of God.

But the grace of God is not magic. It is not fiction. It is not God pretending we are fine when we are not. It is a work that He does in us and through us with His unlimited power focused on doing and fulfilling the will of God the Father in and through us. We must cooperate.

Noah had to work hard for a long, long time, and as a result, he was saved by grace! Now the Lord is building another ark, which is the body of Christ, and we are like the planks in Noah's ark. And the Lord is going to restore everything in a new creation. This is very interesting. Noah's ark is a beautiful picture of what is coming now.

In Matthew 24, the Lord says that when He returns, it will be as in the days of Noah: *For as they were in the days before the flood, eating and drinking, marrying and giving in marriage, until the day that Noah entered into the ark, and they knew not until the flood came and took them all away.* The strongest preaching of Noah was not so much from his words as from his deeds. He started making a huge ark when it had never even rained. The people decided he was crazy, when in fact he was the only sane person on the planet! But he ended up with a family that believed God and believed him.

14a. *Make thee an ark of cedar trees;*

Later, the furniture of the tabernacle of God was also made of cedar. Cedar is a wood that is very resistant to rot, and the bugs do not like it. They say that, high in the snow-covered mountains, Noah's ark is still there (see my friend Dudley Thomas's account http://www.youtube.com/watch?v=klFUHpf-Pmk), despite the fact that the ice melts, exposing the ark to the elements.

> *It is still God's plan to cut off that which is corrupt and to multiply what is righteous and perfect.*

14b. *rooms shalt thou make in the ark and shalt reconcile it within and without covering it over with pitch* [Hebrew "ransom" or "atonement"].

15. *And this is the fashion of which thou shalt make it: The length of the ark shall be three hundred cubits, the breadth of it fifty cubits, and the height of it thirty cubits.*

The number 300 can be deciphered in the mathematics of God in various ways, but the simplest is that 300 is 3 multiplied by 100. In Scripture, 100 is the plan of God – Noah apparently spent 100 years constructing the ark and raising triplets! And 3 is the number that symbolizes being fruitful from the third day of creation. So this was the plan of God to multiply Noah who was perfect in his generations. This was the first purpose of the ark length, because God was going to wipe out those who were producing the evil fruit of violence, wickedness, and corruption.

It is still God's plan to cut off that which is corrupt and to multiply what is righteous and perfect. Everything that originates from Adam is corrupt, but what comes from Christ is perfect. It is so simple. Where will we be found? Will we be among those who were seeking women and giving women, dominating and being the giants and nobility of the earth until it all comes to an abrupt end? Or will we be found among those who, in anticipation, found the grace of God, helped construct the ark, and found refuge there? The ark is the symbol of the true work of God on the earth. This time it is not with planks but with human beings.

The breadth of it fifty cubits. Fifty refers to Pentecost and the power of the Spirit of God. Five is the number that indicates grace and mercy. It is multiplied by ten, which is the Law, because only God can fulfill His will and His law in us. And this is done by mercy, by grace, and by the intervention of God. The Holy Spirit is given not for us to work our own silliness with what God gives us. The Holy Spirit is given so we can learn to be faithful with little things now, in order to receive the fullness of the inheritance later. To be able to manage this inheritance, we must be disciplined now by God as sons of God, because when God has sons and loves them, Scripture says He also disciplines them. This is what the width of the ark indicates. So we have the length and the breadth. The height is thirty cubits. The cubit is the measurement taken of the distance from the elbow to the tips of the fingers of a typical man. The Lord Jesus is the standard for us. And the number thirty in Scripture refers to maturity and perfection.

Methuselah lived 969 years. He was in his 970th year when he died and did not make it to his birthday. If he had lived another thirty years, which symbolizes maturity, he would have been one thousand years old, which symbolizes absolute perfection and plenitude. But none of the patriarchs lived that long. Chapter 20 of Revelation describes the first resurrection of those who will live and reign with Christ for one thousand years. Adam was unable to reach this age, and none of the ancients could either, because they decided to do what they considered to be good and to judge what they considered to be evil. Those who leave all of this to the Lord Jesus and who overcome will be qualified for the promise of Revelation 20 to live the one thousand years, reigning with the Lord Jesus.

The epistle to the Ephesians is very clear. It says that the body of Christ has *nourishment that every connecting bond supplies, by the operation of each member,* and that the time will come when *we all come forth in the unity of the faith and of the knowledge of the Son of God unto a perfect man, unto the measure of the coming of age of the Christ.* This is old terminology referring to the coming of age at thirty when the fullness of the inheritance would be given by the father. When the Lord Jesus was about thirty years of age and He was being baptized, the heavens were opened and the Spirit without measure descended upon Him like a dove. This is what God wants for the entire body of Christ. So we will continue with the ark.

16. *A window shalt thou make to the ark,*

There was only one window, to be able to send and receive the dove. The ark had no more windows. The only window was for a link with the Holy Spirit, and the Holy Spirit would not land on muddy ground. It had to be dry and clean with growing greenery, or He would not be happy. For those who are seeking a true baptism in the Holy Spirit, remember this. For the Lord to baptize us in the Holy Spirit, it is necessary for us to convince Him of something – that we have truly received His Word, that we truly want to listen to Him, and that we truly desire to be under His government and discipline.

> 16. *A window shalt thou make to the ark, and in a cubit shalt thou finish it above; and the door of the ark shalt thou set in the side thereof; with lower, second, and third stories shalt thou make it.*

As mentioned before, these stories represent the three feasts: Passover, Pentecost, and Tabernacles.

17. And, behold, I, even I, do bring a flood of waters upon the earth, to destroy all flesh, in which is the spirit of life, from under heaven; and every thing that is in the earth shall die.

In the symbols of God, the earth is Israel and the church (the people of God). The sea refers to unconverted nations (Gentiles). The judgment of Noah affected the land; it did not affect the sea. The judgment of Noah did not kill the fish; it did not kill the marine life. It killed everything that had breath, the spirit of life that was on land. It killed birds and everything that walked on the land. The Lord says that *judgment begins from the house of God.* It is possible that the Lord is going to commence a judgment soon, and it will not begin upon godless nations. The judgment will commence upon those who claim to represent God. This is where it will begin. There are many who are misrepresenting the Lord and He is about to do something about it. *Everything that is in the earth shall die,* but it also says:

18. But with thee I will establish my covenant; and thou shalt come into the ark, thou and thy sons and thy wife and thy sons' wives with thee.

19. And of every living thing of all flesh, two of every sort shall thou bring into the ark, to keep them alive with thee; they shall be male and female.

20. Of fowls after their kind and of beasts after their kind, of every animal of the earth after its kind, two of every sort shall come unto thee, to keep them alive.

The animals, the birds, the ones that would come unto Noah are the ones that would live. And the ones that did not like Noah would die. Isn't this interesting? The final judgment will be a lot different from what many people think. Many think the final judgment will be determined by such things as: Who practiced the sacraments? Who prayed the sinner's prayer? Who came forward and had the pastor pray for them? Who prayed in tongues? Who did miracles? Who raised their hand when everyone had their eyes shut? But it may not necessarily be like that. Many will even say, *Lord, Lord, have we not prophesied in thy name? and in thy name have cast out devils? and in thy name done many wonderful works?* And the Lord will say, *I never knew you; depart from me, ye that work iniquity.* They were not His sons. He knew who they were, but they were not His sons. They went wild with gifts and ministries yet did not allow themselves to be disciplined by God. And for God, they were spiritual bastards (Deuteronomy 23:2; Hebrews 12:7, 8).

> *...the final state of each person is determined by how they treated the real representatives of God.*

Look at what the Scriptures say – that the final state of each person is determined by how they treated the real representatives of God.

Matthew 10

40. *He that receives you receives me, and he that receives me receives him that sent me.*

41. *He that receives a prophet in the name of a prophet shall receive a prophet's reward, and he that receives a righteous man in the name of a righteous man shall receive a righteous man's reward.*

Those who receive someone sent by the Lord receive the Lord. The person who receives a prophet because he is a prophet will receive the reward of a prophet. On the final day, some will be separated from the presence of God and thrown into the second death, and they will say, "Why? We did so many good things." And the Lord will say, "No, you did nothing good."

Matthew 25

41. *Then he shall also say to those who shall be on the left hand, Depart from me, ye cursed, into eternal fire, prepared for the devil and his angels;*

42. *for I was hungry, and ye gave me no food; I was thirsty, and ye gave me no drink;*

43. *I was a stranger, and ye took me not in; naked, and ye clothed me not; sick and in prison, and ye visited me not.*

44. *Then they shall also answer him, saying, Lord, when did we see thee hungry or thirsty or a stranger or naked or sick or in prison and did not minister unto thee?*

45. *Then he shall answer them, saying, Verily I say unto you, Inasmuch as ye did it not to one of the least of my brothers, ye did it not to me.*

46. *And they shall go away into eternal punishment, but the righteous into eternal life.*

This is not based on religious acts. On that day, the Lord is not going to ask anyone how many religious services they attended. He won't need to know who thought up good social works and helped orphans and prisoners. If they did not have the Spirit of God, they had no discernment. What if many people did a lot of these types of things but they do not qualify because none of those that they helped were really the brothers of the Lord?

In the days of Noah, surely there were many people sawing lumber, preparing wood planks, and making a lot of pretty things with the wood. And although they thought that their works were good, and even though they were very proud of the quality of their carpentry, the only carpentry that was worthwhile was the work that God ordered done.

We do not know if the ark was pretty in comparison to the rest of the craftsmanship of that time. The only thing we know is that it worked. The planks remained reconciled and sealed. The structure of the rooms and the three levels was strong enough to pass through all those immense waves that surrounded the earth.

I spoke with someone who knew of a computer model that could calculate the kind of waves that would have occurred with no continents or landmasses in the way, and with the strong tides that would have resulted due to an unchecked lunar pull. They came to the conclusion that the dimensions of Noah's ark were the only possible dimensions of a vessel that could have survived.

If Noah would have said, "This is too big a project. I am just going to make it two hundred cubits long instead of three hundred," the ark would probably have capsized. What if it would have been made wider or narrower or higher or lower? Noah obeyed God and it worked. And the animals that came and accepted Noah were the ones that lived. In the ark that is coming, which is the family of God, the family of the Lord Jesus, any person who receives one of the true sons (or daughters) of God has possibilities (in Christ there is no male or female; see Galatians 3:28).

It is not necessary that everyone understand everything. The only thing necessary is to receive the messenger or representative sent by God. In so doing, that person also receives the one who sent them. The Lord said to His disciples when He sent them out that anyone who received them received Him, and anyone who received Him received His Father who sent Him. That is why He told them not to wander from house to house. This concept of judgment is very different, but here is the example:

Genesis 6

18. *But with thee I will establish my covenant; and thou shalt come into the ark, thou and thy sons and thy wife and thy sons' wives with thee.*

19. *And of every living thing of all flesh, two of every sort shalt thou bring into the ark, to keep them alive with thee; they shall be male and female.*

20. *Of fowls after their kind and of beasts after their kind, of every animal of the earth after its kind, two of every sort shall come unto thee, to keep them alive.*

21. *And take thou unto thee of all food that is eaten, and thou shalt gather it to thee; and it shall be for food for thee and for them.*

22. *Thus did Noah; according to all that God commanded him, so did he.*

The animals that came to Noah were received, and Noah was the one who had the food. The Lord says that we are in a time of judgment that begins from the house of God (1 Peter 4:17), and the Lord will make the provision for this time. Another picture of this is Joseph in Egypt. The famine lasted for seven years, but in the years of plenty leading up to this time, Joseph and the pharaoh who put him in charge were the only ones who really knew what was about to happen. No one else stored up any provisions. Joseph saved his brothers after two years of famine. They would not have survived the next five years without Joseph.

Genesis 7

1. *And the LORD said unto Noah, Enter thou and all thy house into the ark; for thee have I seen righteous before me in this generation.*

If Noah had not been righteous, it would have been difficult to judge the rest of the world, because the rest of the world could have said no one can be righteous. And this is what they say in many places: "No one can be just; no one can be upright." The Bible says that Noah was righteous and perfect in his genera-tion, and therefore, he found grace with God. Grace is not a covering for corruption to allow the person to continue being corrupt. Noah found grace because he wanted to do things God's way. Noah wanted God to order his house, for God to order his family and children, and for God to order his work. As surely as he had been faithful in small things, now God put him in charge of the major project that was going to save all those who would be saved from the flood. And it is the same now, except that now it is even more important.

2. *Of every clean animal thou shalt take to thee seven pairs, the male and his female; but of animals that are not clean, two, the male and his female.*

3. *Of fowls also of the heavens by seven pairs, the male and the female; to keep seed alive upon the face of all the earth.*

4. *For yet in seven days, I will cause it to rain upon the earth forty days and forty nights; and every sub-stance that I have made I will destroy from off the face of the earth.*

5. *And Noah did according unto all that the LORD commanded him.*

The Lord told Noah to start getting everything into the ark seven days before the event. And the Bible says that for the Lord one day is as a thousand years and a thousand years are as a day. Creation started going haywire six thousand years ago, six prophetic days ago, and we are now entering the seventh prophetic day.

For the past six thousand years, God has gathered people to make up part of His ark of salvation. The Lord says that from righteous Abel who was killed by his brother, to Enoch who walked with God and did not see death because the Lord took him, and on to the present, He has been forming a company of over-comers who are now with the Lord (Hebrews 11). *God having provided some better thing for us, that they without us should not be made per-fect* (speaking of resurrection).

> *He wants us to be part of Him and do what He wants, not try to use Him to get what we want.*

So where are we? Six prophetic days are passed and one day is left. On the seventh day, everything was completed. God finished the first creation on the seventh day. He worked on the seventh day until everything was perfect and then He rested.

We are entering the seventh millennium when the Lord has promised that there are going to be some who will reign with Him a thousand years. And in all this, when the thousand years are ended, the book of Revelation says that the first heavens and earth were not found because now there are new heavens and a new earth. Second Peter 3:13 says this is where righteousness dwells.

So what does the Lord desire? He wants us to be in the ark and He is the ark. He wants us to be part of Him and do what He wants, not try to use Him to get what we want. Perhaps many people thought that God would help them in their daily concerns when all of a sudden the flood took them all away. The only ones who were saved were those who spent maybe one hundred years or more dedicated only to what God had told them to do.

5. *And Noah did according unto all that the LORD commanded him.*

6. *And Noah was six hundred years old when the flood of waters was upon the earth.*

His grandfather died and the flood came.

7. *And Noah went in and his sons and his wife and his sons' wives with him into the ark because of the waters of the flood.*

8. *Of clean animals and of animals that are not clean and of fowls and of every thing that moves upon the earth,*

9. *there went in two by two unto Noah into the ark, the male and the female, as God had commanded Noah.*

10. *And it came to pass after seven days* [on the seventh day] *that the waters of the flood were upon the earth.*

God sent them into the ark, and on the seventh day the waters came. God has placed His plan of salvation from before the foundation of the world, and in the seventh day, the Lord says that the world is going to come to an end. In the seventh millennium, the world is going to end, and only those who are found in the life of the Lord are going to survive.

11. *In the six hundredth year of Noah's life in the second month, the seventeenth day of the month, the same day were all the fountains of the great deep broken up, and the windows of the heavens were opened.*

12. *And there was rain upon the earth forty days and forty nights.*

Forty also refers to the desert, with testing. When the Lord cuts things off, He cuts off that which is of no useful purpose. In this example, He cut off all humanity that lived according to the flesh. And all that was left was the one family that chose to be ordered by God. Noah is a symbol of Christ. The family of Christ in these final days is much larger than the family of Noah was then.

In the second month, the seventeenth day of the month. I am going to condense this. The waters lasted 150 days. In the book of Revelation, when the fifth trumpet is sounded, there is a judgment of five months or 150 days. This is a very interesting parallel. When the waters began to recede, it was on the seventh month on the seventeenth day. On the calendar of God, the sacred year begins with the seventh month (see Leviticus 23:24-36). The seventeenth day is the third day of the Feast of Tabernacles.

What did God want? He wanted to make a covenant with a special family that would seek the way of God, and He sealed this covenant with a rainbow (Hebrew "arc"). The rainbow gave special privileges not only to Noah but also to all creation. When you see the rainbow, what do you see? From earth, all you see is the arc stretching 180 degrees from the horizon back to the horizon. From the heavens, however, you do not see a rainbow (half a circle); you see the entire circle. I have seen this many times from an airplane. And from the air when you see what would be a rainbow if you were on the ground, it is no longer called a rainbow; it is called a glory. A glory is a perfect rainbow; it has no beginning and it has no end. The intensity of the colors is also much greater when seen from above.

Surely there are many parallels in many parts of the Scriptures, and surely the Lord will reveal His secrets to those He loves. And there are many things in God that cannot be taught. The Ten Commandments can be taught, and also the Lord's Prayer, the Beatitudes, etc. It is one thing to get students to repeat these things like parrots; it is another thing for the Lord to reveal what He indeed desires. This picture of Noah is very interesting because of all that is in the picture. Everything is in its proper place. All this is prophetic and is about to happen on another higher level.

> *It is one thing to get students to repeat these things like parrots; it is another thing for the Lord to reveal what He indeed desires.*

Genesis 8

1. *And God remembered Noah, and every living thing, and all the animals that were with him in the ark; and God made a wind to pass over the earth, and the waters ceased;*

Wind, spirit, and breath are all the same word in Hebrew.

2. *the fountains also of the deep and the windows of the heavens were stopped, and the rain from heaven was restrained;*

3. *and the waters turned back and forth upon the earth, and after the end of the hundred and fifty days the waters were abated.*

Back and forth, back and forth. There were surely some huge waves.

4. *And the ark rested in the seventh month, on the seventeenth day of the month, upon the mountains of Ararat.*

5. *And the waters decreased continually until the tenth month; in the tenth month, on the first day of the month, the tops of the mountains were seen.*

6. *And it came to pass at the end of forty days that Noah opened the window of the ark which he had made,*

7. *and he sent forth a raven, which went to and fro until the waters were dried up from off the earth.*

8. *Also he sent forth a dove from him to see if the waters were abated from off the face of the ground,*

9. *but the dove found no rest for the sole of her foot, and she returned unto him into the ark, for the waters were still upon the face of the whole earth. Then he put forth his hand and took her and pulled her in unto him into the ark.*

10. *And he waited yet another seven days, and again he sent forth the dove out of the ark,*

11. *and the dove came in to him in the evening, and, behold, in her mouth was an olive leaf plucked off, so Noah knew that the waters were abated from off the earth.*

12. *And he stayed yet other seven days and sent forth the dove, which returned not again unto him any more.*

13. *And it came to pass in the six hundredth and first year of Noah, in the first month, the first day of the month, the waters were dried up from off the earth, and Noah removed the covering of the ark and looked and, behold, the face of the ground was dry.*

The ark was covered all this time. They only had the one window. All of this is very symbolic of what God does with us.

And just as there may be a final judgment, this is also a symbol of what God wants to do in the individual lives of all of us. The Lord wants to apply judgment and strip away all that is not useful pertaining to the old man. The old man is not useful to God. The old man certainly does evil all the time. He is never good. Humanism is sadly mistaken. If we want to do good, we must return to God, and if we return to God, He will pass us through judgment, and He can do this on an individual level.

A friend came by who had been listening to these messages over the past several years, but things had not been going so well for him. He had trouble with his business, problems with debts, with bills, with workers, with many things, and he came to ask me what was going on. I had to answer, "Nothing. Your case is typical. This is normal for anyone who is really called to enter the Feast of Tabernacles and experience the true presence of God."

What do you think it was like for those 150 days inside that ark? What were those impressive waves like? Did they ever come close to overturning the ark? What if the structure started to come apart? What was happening with the elephants and lions in the midst of such a spectacular storm? No, Noah rested when the judgment came. Noah means "rest." Scripture says it will be as in the days of Noah. How will it be? How were the days of Noah?

Matthew 24

38. *For as they were in the days before the flood, eating and drinking, marrying and giving in marriage, until the day that Noah entered into the ark,*

39. *and they knew not until the flood came and took them all away; so shall also the coming of the Son of man be.*

They were giving away women and taking women; this is something that only God is qualified to do. He is our creator and this is His right. In the book of Proverbs, it says that when the Lord gives someone a wife, this is extremely important and is to be very highly esteemed. Many other Scriptures confirm this (Proverbs 19:14).

To go from one woman to another and mix this all up was one of the grave problems of the ancient world. And they were doing it right up until the time that Noah and his family entered the ark.

Also, on a spiritual level, sometimes God refers to entire congregations of people as women. In Revelation, there is a great harlot who seems to have many daughters. The prophetic Scriptures are laced with references to spiritual infidelity and promiscuity and the consequences. How many people are still skipping around from one congregation to the next, trying to find the most benefits for themselves instead of seriously listening to the Lord?

> 39. *and they knew not until the flood came and took them all away; so shall also the coming of the Son of man be.*

> 40. *Then shall two be in the field; the one shall be taken and the other left.*

The one that is taken shall be taken, but how? Where? And the one that is left will be stuck right in the midst of the so-called great tribulation. In the days of Noah how was it? Who was taken? All those of the ancient world. Who was left? Noah and his family who went right through the tribulation because they were in the ark, and in the ark they had the grace of God (full provision for every need).

And in the days of the coming of the Son of Man, there will be two in the field, and it says that one shall be taken and the other left. Only two men. One represents Adam and the other represents Christ. The real Christians are the ones who are going to be left because the meek shall inherit the earth (Matthew 5:5). And those who are taken will be the sons of Adam. In Numbers 24 it says, *there shall come a Star out of Jacob, and a Sceptre shall rise out of Israel and shall smite all the corners of Moab and destroy all the sons of Seth* (Seth is the heir of Adam; see Genesis 5:3).

41. *Two women shall be grinding at the mill; the one shall be taken and the other left.*

There is a true church and a false church, and the false church shall be wiped out and taken away.

42. *Watch therefore, for ye know not what hour your Lord doth come.*

43. *But know this that if the husband of the house knew in what watch the thief would come, he would watch and would not suffer his house to be broken into.*

44. *Therefore be ye also ready; the Son of man is to come in the hour that ye think not.*

45. *Who then is the faithful and prudent slave, whom his lord has made ruler over his household to give them food in due season?*

46. *Blessed is that slave whom his lord when he comes shall find so doing.*

47. *Verily I say unto you, That he shall make him ruler over all his goods.*

48. *But and if that evil slave shall say in his heart, My lord delays his coming,*

49. *and shall begin to smite his fellowslaves and even to eat and drink with the drunken,*

50. *the lord of that slave shall come in a day when he does not look for him and in an hour that he is not aware of*

51. *and shall cut him off and appoint him his portion with the hypocrites; there shall be weeping and gnashing of teeth.*

Would it not be much better to allow the Lord to do His work in us now and take away anything in us that is not pleasing to Him?

What is the raven? The raven is a carrion bird. It eats that which is dead and rotten. The Lord wants to clean everything up, and He can begin with water (*the washing of water by the word*).

> *The fig tree is putting forth leaves all over the place, so we know that we are coming down the final stretch.*

But the time comes when He lets the raven loose and it does not come back. It eats that which is dead, the carnal part that God wants dead. God wants this carnal part dead even if the ravens have to eat it.

But the dove cannot rest until the olive is putting forth leaves and the ground is dry. The dove did not bring leaves from the fig tree (which is a symbol of the religion of man as man attempts to cover himself; see Genesis 3:7). The Lord cursed the fig tree and said that no one would ever eat fruit from her again (Mark 11:14, 21). But He also said that when the fig tree puts forth its leaves, we can know that the time of the return of the Lord in judgment is near. Because the religion of men is putting forth a flurry of leaves as men try to cover themselves but are not putting forth good fruit, no one can live off the fruit that they are producing. The fig tree is putting forth leaves all over the place, so we know that we are coming down the final stretch.

But if the Lord is dealing with us as individuals, after He does away with what is carnal in us, He wants the good olive (the good olive is the life of Christ in us) to begin to sprout again. The Lord Jesus is called the branch (or sprout), and He wants to do this (sprout) in us. He wants the Holy Spirit (the dove) to return to Jesus (Noah) with the tender leaf, with the sample that the earth (which is us) is beginning to reproduce in us the right kind of life – His life planted in us. And when the ground is dry, the dove can leave the hand of Noah (the hand of Jesus) and remain on us.

Before this, the dove could only flutter here and there, and many of us have only had these sporadic light touches by the Holy Spirit. But we need the fullness of the presence of God. This is the same as the baptism (saturation) in the Holy Spirit, the true baptism into the Holy Spirit that can only be accomplished by the Lord Jesus. John the Baptist could baptize in water, and this is a beautiful symbol, but it remains just a symbol (see Matthew 3:11; 1 Corinthians 1:14-17). Jesus wants to take us from the symbol into reality. And the reality is something that only He can do. He baptizes in the Holy Spirit and in fire, and the final judgment is by fire.

The works of each of us will be tested by fire – our gold, silver, and precious stones, or our wood, hay, stubble, and tares. Many ask me what they ought to do. They think that we will organize them into a prayer group or a ladies' group or a men's group or a group that will minister somewhere, and some get upset when we do not do this. It is not that we are unable to invent things like this; it is that I do not want to be doing what everyone was doing before the flood. They were doing what they thought was good, but God did not approve of any of it. The only ones who were approved were doing what God had expressly ordered them to do. And I do not believe that I am in the capacity of being able to order your lives, because I have a big enough problem with my own. Rather, I am in need of your prayers that I might depend only on the Lord each and every day for direction.

The beautiful thing about all of this is that we do not in actuality prepare the messages. The messages we deliver are born of the Spirit and flow not only out of my mouth but also out of the mouths of many of you who are preaching in the same manner. And just as we walk each week with the Lord, 24/7 practicing His wishes, so Noah walked with God and look what happened. He found grace and was found righteous and perfect in the midst of a perverse generation! And his family was saved and went safely with him right through the midst of the judgment!

The idea that I have, the vision I have, that which burns in my heart, is that each and every one of you will be led directly by the Spirit of God, that you will walk with the Lord, and that the Lord will be able to put you to work doing what He wants. In order for this to happen, we must open our hearts and our minds so He can enter and have His way inside of us. Notice that some of you who had many questions a few months or a few years ago now have gotten over this. Why? Because the Lord is answering your questions directly. This is why we have no formal counseling sessions. If someone is in need, we are here; many of us are here.

What does the Lord want? He wants to respond to these situations. He is the only one who has the solution, and this is why we do not tell anyone to come to us for counsel on a regular weekly basis. We will not be anyone's "spiritual direc-tor." I understand that in special cases it is necessary to give advice, but you cannot live your lives based on my counsel. The best that can happen with my advice is to help troubleshoot a problem, but the only lasting solution is for you to be in direct contact with the Lord.

The Lord wants to govern your life. He wants your conscience connected to the Holy Spirit so your relationship with Him is so intense that if something is wrong you will not be at peace. If you have ever experienced the peace that passes understanding and if this peace should ever be lifted, it is and should be very troubling. So instead of getting a psychiatric prescription, God wants us to repent of any sin and make sure that He is really in charge of our lives.

Let the Lord be the one to motivate us and indicate what must be done to return to true peace. True peace is useful in the midst of the storm. Noah did not get bent out of shape. The Scripture says that after 150 days of something wilder than the most spectacular roller coaster we can imagine, while packed into close quarters with more wild animals than a circus, God remembered Noah and his family and all the animals. And while they were still packed into the ark, God was preparing the land so they could come out into freedom. And all those evil people who had mocked them and caused them so much trouble were nowhere to be seen. They were rotting. They were at the bottom of the sea. The ravens were eating them. Then there was a new earth, the dove of God was free, and the good olive was flourishing. God is going to do this again. He is going to make new heavens and a new earth, and He is preparing very special people to be with Him in all of this.

Let us pray

Lord, we give you thanks. We ask, Lord, that we might understand this message – not just the words, not just a mental acceptation – but that this message might enter profoundly into our very being and into our heart that we might be ready and available for service in your ark, regarding the food and regarding the animals, that we, Lord, might become a great sign for whoever is still out there without spiritual life, acting like a human beast, so they might come and touch reality and enter into salvation. Lord, we ask that this will happen before it is too late. Amen.

CHAPTER 2

The Altar and the Gospel

⎯⎯⎯⎯⎯⎯ ⊥ ⎯⎯⎯⎯⎯⎯

When the word being preached is anointed and on target, it is easier to receive or to accept. At least, it is sweet to our taste even though it might be a bitter purge to our stomach. Nevertheless, we must be prepared for the moment when someone takes the microphone and says something that is completely absurd. This could happen; it happens everywhere. And when this happens, we all need to have the wisdom and anointing from God to handle the situation, because we are still in the realm where we see as the apostle describes – *For now we see as through a mirror in darkness* (1 Corinthians 13:12).

The gifts that we have from God still function in the realm of "in part"; for we are not yet in the realm of absolute perfection, although sometimes this may happen for short periods of time. Yet perfection is the goal. So if something is said that is a mistake, it is necessary to have the discernment from the Spirit of God to eat the meat and spit out the bones!

If we are asking good things from the Lord, He promises to give them to us. So if we are going to preach or teach, it is necessary to be convinced that this is what God wants us to say. We should be willing to give our lives for the truth that the Lord has given us. But the fact that someone is willing to give their life for the truth doesn't necessarily mean that everything they say is true. Any one of us could easily have an area of blindness.

In the natural, we all have the same characteristic. All of us can see more or less in a forward arc of 120 degrees, and within this limit we see well. Then there is a peripheral area on each side where we do not see too well. Finally, there is another area behind us where we cannot see at all and where it is not possible for any flesh-and-blood human to see. If we wish to see behind us, we have to turn our head or trust someone who is looking at us head-on who can see what is going on back there. Therefore, if we feel that the Lord is uniting us with another brother who is looking at us from the opposite direction, who is also seeking to be pure of heart as we are, when this brother comes to us and says, "Look, I am seeing something that perhaps you are not seeing," what should we do? It is our duty to pay attention and bring the matter before the Lord.

If the Lord decides to tell us something by using another brother (or sister) when he or she is speaking or writing (even if this comes as a shock because they managed to hit a real sore spot), our initial reaction may be one of pain. We may jump a bit, but afterwards, if we contemplate the problem before the Lord, and the Spirit of God begins to show us that what our brother or sister said was true, we must stand corrected. This is how we can grow.

The theme of this chapter is basic – it is the theme of the altar and the blood. Someone asked, "We heard that you have a meeting over at a certain person's place. Tell me, under what 'covering' are you conducting this meeting?" This person had no bad intent. In the realm that he operated in, he really wanted to know what the covering was, and this was a common question. This person most likely thought that we were going to say, "We are operating under the covering of Apostle so and so or of this or that organization or denomination."

And he was suddenly surprised when my wife simply said, "We are operating under the covering of the Holy Spirit."

And just how does this covering of the Holy Spirit work? It is common for people who say they are operating under the covering of the Holy Spirit to wind up in a lot of trouble. They may be perceived as loose cannons or spiritual lone rangers. Embarrassing situations may arise with no one around to give any answers.

For these and other reasons, committees are formed, apostles are named, and a hierarchical system is developed so these mishaps no longer occur when the name of the Lord is involved. Every time there is a problem, more rules are established to avoid situations getting out of control. And these things function apparently well at the beginning, but after two thousand years, there are more than two thousand major sects all claiming to have "the real apostles."

Fifteen years ago, I was speaking with a brother who I believe is a real apostle. (The word apostle really means one who is sent by the Lord, and when the Lord sends someone, He delegates the authority so the person can represent Him.) This brother had been the target of threats. He decided to go into hiding but was not sure what would happen to the four hundred or so groups that he was managing.

So I said to him, "Well, brother, I have never had that much responsibility, but in the dealings that I have had with a maximum of thirty leaders, what I have proposed to them and what I have proposed concerning myself is that we all be on record privately and publicly with a full commitment to the Lord. We are committed before God and before the people to receive discipline and correction from the Lord as necessary. We all look to the Lord to deal with us directly as He sees fit."

What gives me the most confidence to trust someone in leadership is to have the testimony that God really does deal with that leader with correction and intervention. This gives the basis for trust and is a sign or security that the Lord is directly responsible for that person and ministry. If we have to convene a committee or refer the situation to an "apostle," and if we have to have a detective to keep those who have credentials issued by whatever organization or church under surveillance so no one gets away with anything, this may all prove worthless in the end. (And it would take some pretty good detectives!) The Spirit of God can stop these problems in a flash before they can be manifested in word or deed, when the only evidence is a wrong desire in someone's heart.

> *The Spirit of God can stop these problems in a flash before they can be manifested in word or deed, when the only evidence is a wrong desire in someone's heart.*

Furthermore, if the brethren have to intervene in the correction of someone in particular (there is a procedure outlined in the Bible that speaks of using two or three witnesses, and if that fails, to take it before the congregation), the very fact that there are two or three witnesses of whatever problem (theft, adultery, or something of this nature) means that the ministry of the person in question is severely damaged (even if they repent). It will take a long time to recover (if it is even possible to recover).

On the contrary, the Lord can deal with our hearts directly when there is just a minimal sign of getting off course. He can correct our ministry even before we have committed any outward sign or failure of such magnitude as to bring a bad testimony before the world. So the covering of the Spirit of God is the best covering. The Spirit of God works through human individuals but also intervenes directly.

I was in the city of Minneapolis giving a message at the funeral of Jeanne, the wife of brother Clayt Sonmore. When the service was over, Clayt and I were both invited to visit a group of leaders who specialized in large meetings. One of them had gathered as many as 16,000 people in conventions, and another had groups in many places. These people had submitted themselves to two apostles; the first had just passed away, and the second was on his deathbed. Because of this, they thought they were in danger of being without a "covering" and had invited brother Clayt because they thought that, in him, they would have another "father" or apostle who could be responsible for them.

So brother Clayt stood before them and said, "When I have the anointing of God, it is well and good for you to listen to me and heed what I say – if it really is the voice of God. But the problem is that I do not always have the word of the Lord. So if I speak on my own word and you continue to follow me, we would be like the blind following the blind, and Scripture says that we will all end up in a pit (Matthew 15:14). This applies to all of us. There are times when the Lord speaks clearly through us and there are other times when this is not the case."

Clayt told them he was not going to be their elder brother (leader) because we already have an elder brother who is called the Lord Jesus. He said he would not be their covering apostle because there already is a chief apostle, the same Lord Jesus. He graciously offered to be of service and to be available to answer any question that the Lord might give him the anointing to address, and they would be at liberty to take his advice or to leave it. But he refused to let them name him as their apostle where they would obey everything he said. Clayt did not accept, and

I do not believe that any of us will accept if we are ever offered something similar. The Lord does delegate responsibility, but we have to work within that responsibility according to what the Lord is doing in us. The end of this matter is that it is the Lord who is at liberty to work as He desires.

Therefore, it is extremely important to understand about the altar and the blood, because it is on the altar that the blood is applied, because the life is closely associated with the blood. In the Scriptures, the book of Leviticus says that we are not to eat blood because the life (same word as "soul" in Hebrew) is in the blood (Genesis 9:4; Leviticus 17:11-15). If we want to receive this covering of life of the Spirit of God (because the Spirit of God is the life of Jesus and He orders us to be covered with His Spirit), if we desire to enter in and be hid in the life of Christ which is symbolized in Scripture as a white robe, then we need to leave our own life and our own desires behind.

We cannot continue being the gods of our own lives if we wish to come under the covering of God. This must be resolved at the altar. In the Old Testament they built altars, beginning in the book of Genesis when two brothers each decided to present their offering to the Lord (remember the story). One of the offerings was received and the other was not. God approved the altar and the sacrifice of one and did not approve the altar or the sacrifice of the other. One offered a lamb; the other offered the work of his hands, which was the grain that he had produced.

In Exodus 20, the Lord gave commandments to His people. How did they get the Law and the Ten Commandments written on tablets of stone? They got them because they decided and expressed that they did not desire to hear the voice of the Lord any longer, because if they did, they thought that they would die. So they sent Moses to climb the mountain to hear the voice of God and come back and tell them what God said (Deuteronomy 5:24-27). After Moses went up and came back with the Ten Commandments, the people were already in idolatry with the golden calf. Moses threw down the commandments because they were already broken (Exodus 32:19). It is not possible to fulfill the law of God when we receive it secondhand. The only way to be able to fulfill it is when God Himself writes it on the tablet of our heart and in our mind; this is what the dealing at the altar is for.

After the breaking of the tablets, God gave two warnings to the people regarding the altar:

Exodus 20

23. Ye shall not make with me gods of silver, neither shall ye make unto you gods of gold [and the god of money is still a great temptation before the people of God!].

24. An altar of earth thou shalt make unto me and shalt sacrifice thereon thy burnt offerings and thy peace offerings, thy sheep and thine oxen; in whatever place where I cause my name to be remembered, I will come unto thee, and I will bless thee.

25. And if thou wilt make me an altar of stone, thou shalt not build it of hewn stone; for if thou lift up thy tool upon it, thou hast polluted it.

26. Neither shalt thou go up by steps unto my altar that thy nakedness not be discovered thereon.

The altar in the Old Testament is the equivalent of the gospel in the New Testament. The altar is a place where we can have an encounter with the Lord to make a covenant with Him. And the symbols of the covenant are bread and wine, which in the Old Testament were the symbols of the grain and the blood that were offered upon the altar. The grain (bread) without the blood (wine) is not received by God, and this is where Cain failed. We cannot enter into the provision of God in our own life without forsaking the old life. Cain wanted to enter into the blessing without the blood, and he was not received. Instead of repenting, he became angry and killed his brother.

The first reference to the blood in the Bible appears when Cain killed his brother Abel (Genesis 4:10). The last reference is in the book of Revelation chapter 19 when the Lord, who is called Faithful and True (*And he was clothed in a garment dipped in blood*), comes forth victorious over all the forces of evil. The blood theme is of extreme importance because the problem started with blood and is finished with blood. All of us in our natural state have contributed to or participated in the sin of Cain. Afterward, we partook in the crime of the Jews when they killed the Lord; we did this through our actions, our apathy, and our selfishness. Therefore, we need to be under the covering of the blood of Jesus.

As we noticed in Exodus 20, the conditions cannot be changed. When God puts out stones, we cannot chip away at them. The conditions have to be as God has established. If we attempt to embellish or smooth the stones of the altar, the Word of God says that we are really polluting it. What have we done with the New Testament? We have said that it is not necessary to repent; it is not necessary that the old man die. All we have to do is receive Christ (some say we only have to receive what He did), and when we receive Him, we will receive the best of this world also. Such is the gospel that many preach, when the real gospel of God is a gospel of complete surrender to the Lord.

Neither can we make an altar with gradations, because if we make the altar with gradual steps, our nakedness will be exposed. In other words, if we want to come to the Lord in stages, little by little giving Him a bit of our life today and a little something else tomorrow, and if we think that in this way we can draw near to the altar (by going up some steps one at a time), what we do not give over to the Lord will turn into an enemy target against us. This is what the enemy will shoot at. When someone says, "I am willing to serve the Lord and do what He wants except for such and such," or "I am willing to give up everything except this thing," precisely whatever it is that is being held back becomes the battlefield and the area in which the person will be defeated. And when you are defeated, your shame will be exposed as a bad testimony in front of everyone.

> *God's way is that we surrender our life to Him or we do not. Hot or cold, but not lukewarm.*

Therefore, God's system does not include an altar with steps. God's way is that we surrender our life to Him or we do not. Hot or cold, but not lukewarm. Later in Scripture there is another example.

Ezra 3

3. And they set the altar upon its bases, for fear was upon them because of the peoples of those lands, and they offered burnt offerings upon it unto the LORD, even burnt offerings morning and evening.

Why did they raise up the altar first? Why did they not build the wall first? (The wall was the last thing they built.)

The people had come to restore the city of God, and the first thing they did was to rebuild the altar and begin blood sacrifices. Later they rebuilt the temple, and finally they rebuilt the walls and gates of the city. They knew that the altar involved the covering, and the blood had to be applied in order for them to be covered, because the life is in the blood. If the blood is not applied God's way, if there is no altar according to the way of God, there is no baptism in the Holy Spirit. If there is no baptism in the Holy Spirit, there is no covering or protection.

The real baptism is in the Holy Spirit and in fire (Matthew 3:11; Luke 3:16). The fire on the altar cannot be just any fire. We cannot light an altar with our own fire; the fire must be lit by God. If the fire is not God's fire, the altar will not work and becomes an abomination before the Lord. All of these things are important for us to analyze because for us today, it is necessary to understand that the altar is not a pile of stones on which to kill an animal. The altar is not a specific site; the altar means to make a contract, a covenant with God, according to God's terms and conditions. And for reference, we have the symbols of the Old Covenant.

According to Leviticus 4-7 in the original texts, it says the people had to come to the altar to *offer their sin*. In other versions of the Scriptures, it reads that they are to bring a *sin offering*. The original does not mention a sin offering. It says we are to *offer our sin*. The altar and the application of the blood are not so we can continue in our sins under some strange covering of the grace of God (like a work of magic). The altar is so we can come out clean without sin. So it is necessary that we understand how they were to do it.

They were to take a bullock and put their hands on it. This animal then became the sin, so they had to take the sin to the altar and bleed it to death. In this instant, the person who was making this sacrifice had to be there with their hands on the head of the animal, helping the priest to kill the "sin."

In the same manner, we are to offer our sin with the help of the Lord Jesus, for He is now the only mediator between God and man. He is the one who helps us take our sin, kill it, bleed it to death, and drain the life out of it, so the sin will have no more power over us now or in the future. These animals could be dangerous; they could kick or gore anyone who was not careful.

The altar is the place where we can have a direct encounter with our Lord Jesus. It can be wherever we are – in the house, in a meeting, anywhere. The physical site is not important. What is important now is that we have an encounter with the Lord Jesus, and that we surrender our sin to Him so He can help us kill it until the sin no longer has power over us.

There is another sacrifice symbolized by a ram. Some Bible versions translated this as a "guilt offering," but in the original, it says that we should *offer our guilt*. After the Lord helps us kill our sin, the enemy wants to tell us, "You cannot have a personal relationship with God. You can't have communion with God. You can't behave as a son of God. You are not worthy to have a ministry serving God." He will go on and on raking us over the coals regarding our past failures. So what does God want to do? He wants to kill our guilt so we do not have it anymore. And in the book of Leviticus this is symbolized by a second sacrifice that could be a ram.

After getting rid of sin and guilt, there is a third sacrifice described that was made on the altar called the sacrifice of peace ("peace offering" in some Bible versions). This sacrifice, according to the original, is to be made in holocaust. This is where this term "holocaust" is introduced in Scripture, and it means a sacrifice that is completely burnt up in the fire of God.

All that is left after a sacrifice of peace offered in holocaust to the Lord is a pile of ashes and the oil or fat that would run off the altar and be collected in a special place. This is why Isaiah was inspired to write:

Isaiah 61

3. to order in Zion those that mourn, to give unto them beauty [glory] *for **ashes**, the **oil** of joy for mourning, the garment* [covering] *of praise for the spirit of heaviness; that they might be called trees of righteousness, the planting of the LORD, that he might be glorified* (emphasis added).

Once sin and guilt are dead and gone, we can offer ourselves to the Lord and enter a life of victory. The sacrifice of peace on the altar of God symbolizes the person willing and available for whatever God wants because they are not their own; they have been bought with a great price.

The fact that we can come out from under all the weight of sin and guilt is presented as salvation that we do not deserve and that we cannot buy with any of our own works. But it carries a tremendous price because the Lord paid with His life. If we enter into the covering provided by His life, we should not return to our own life. If we are identified with the death of Jesus, then we must leave our pride, arrogance, and obstinacy behind so we might comply with His will. These are the conditions of the altar.

Romans 5

10. For if, when we were enemies, we were reconciled with God by the death of his Son, much more, now reconciled, we shall be saved by his life.

The altar is for a complete surrender to the Lord, not a partial surrender. When a complete surrender takes place, something interesting happens regarding the holocaust, which really means "ascending." This is the same word used when Jacob saw (in a dream) a ladder from the earth up to heaven, and the angels of God were ascending and descending (holocaust-ing).

When we offer our lives, when we offer the good that we have received from God, when we offer a clean life before the Lord, then the heavens will open for us, and the way for us to have communion with God will open, not just with the Lord Jesus but also with the Father. This means access to the throne of God, and the Scriptures say that we can now come boldly before the throne of God to make our petitions known (1 John 5:14). If two or three of us are in accord in the name (in the nature) of the Lord, our petition will be granted (Matthew 18:19, 20).

If we are busy making petitions that have not been conceded, maybe we are not in agreement with others who are flowing in the nature of God, or maybe we are not really asking in the name (nature) of God. These petitions may be made in the name of God, not in our own name.

...sometimes we do not realize that the Lord Jesus wants to be born in each of our hearts.

And because this altar is to take us out of the nature of Adam by doing away with the old man, we will have access to a new nature in Jesus, where the heavens will open for us. The altar enables the celestial presence of Jesus, which comes by the Holy Spirit, to enter our lives and cover us.

This was promised to the Virgin Mary; she would have a child without ever having known a man. And the angel said unto her: *The Holy Spirit shall come upon thee, and the power of the Highest shall overshadow* [cover] *thee* (Luke 1:35).

Because of this, she had a child and called His name Jesus, and you know the rest of the story. But sometimes we do not realize that the Lord Jesus wants to be born in each of our hearts. This functions the same way as it did with Mary. When the presence of Jesus is in a person, He can be extended to another person. When the Holy Spirit came over Mary and the Lord Jesus was conceived inside of her, she went right away over to her cousin Elizabeth's (who was six months pregnant with John the Baptist). When Elizabeth saw her, she felt the baby inside of her jump for joy. In this instant, John the Baptist was "baptized" three months before he was born, and his mother Elizabeth was too (Luke 1:41, 44)! After this, the Holy Spirit came over Zacharias, his father (who had become dumb months before), and he opened his mouth and prophesied.

How did Mary qualify for such an honor? When the angel Gabriel came to her with such a strange and dangerous proposition, she replied, *Behold the handmaid of the Lord; be it unto me according to thy word* (Luke 1:38).

When we surrender on the altar of God to do His will, however He commands, the way for the covering of the Holy Spirit opens up. This covering of the Holy Spirit can affect others who are close to us. What is happening today in the church? Too many are under the covering of man and are not under the covering of the Holy Spirit.

The covering of man has many limitations. The disciple cannot be greater than his teacher (Matthew 10:24), and if you have man as your teacher, you will never surpass that teacher. But if our teacher is the Lord, Scripture says that when we become like our Master we will be perfect (Matthew 10:25). This can only happen if we remain under the covering of the Holy Spirit. Apostles and prophets, as the governmental body in the church, are only mentioned in two or three verses in this context. The blood and the altar are mentioned in more than 350 verses each. This is about the same frequency as other important terms like peace, justice, and righteousness.

Philippians 3

7. But those things which were gain to me, I counted loss for Christ.

8. *And doubtless I even count all things as loss for the excellency of the knowledge of Christ Jesus my Lord, for whom I have suffered the loss of all things and do count them but dung, that I may win Christ*

9. *and be found in him, not having my own righteousness, which is of the law, but that which is through the faith of Christ, the righteousness which is of God by faith:*

Note that the Scripture does not say *the faith in Christ*. Paul is referring to the fact that he is now operating in *the faith of Christ*. Our faith can get us to the altar, but if we want to fulfill what God requires, it is necessary for the faith *of* Christ to begin to operate in our lives, and this will only happen if we have entered into Him. The death of Christ can cover all of us. Why? Because when someone dies, all accusations against the dead person cease.

If the government has an indictment against anyone to take away their goods or to accuse them of a crime, the case can continue and be judged for as long as the person is alive. But if the person dies, the case is cancelled and cannot be continued. No judge in any country will continue a criminal case against a dead person. The maximum penalty that a court can exact (if the laws of the country provide for it) is the death penalty, and if the person is already dead, there is no further penalty that the court can exact!

So what is the purpose of the altar? It is to offer ourselves so we can have the opportunity to die now instead of later. By means of the altar, we can enter into a covenant with God and say unto Him, "Here I am. I surrender. I give up. I desist." Then the Lord will apply the blood over us, kill the sin, kill the guilt, and receive us as an offering, as a living holocaust. He will open the heavens toward us, and our lives will not be lived for our own self; we will live for Him. We are no longer our own. We belong to Him. We were bought by His death. This is the good news of the gospel.

Revelation 19

11. *And I saw the heaven open.*

This is what happens when we have entered by the altar of God; the heavens open. This holocaust of our life becomes like Jacob's ladder connecting heaven and earth, where our petitions are heard and responded to because we are not asking according to the desires and concupiscence of our flesh, but according to the will of God, which is much different. But even with this, we must be in accord with two or three other people who are also functioning in the nature of God because we still have blind spots where we do not see things. The Lord does not give a complete revelation to any of us as individuals because He wants to form us into a body of many members where we all need and depend on one another.

> *He wants to form us into a body of many members where we all need and depend on one another.*

11. *and behold a white horse; and he that was seated upon him was called Faithful and True, and in righteousness he judges and makes war.*

Israel was not to trust in horses because the horse is the symbol of the strength of the natural man. But here is a white horse, a clean, natural man, and Christ is seated upon this horse and goes to war. We are not to trust horses (the natural man), but He wants to make us into part of the white horse that He is going to ride. Here He is going to control us, and we are going to take Him to the battle, instead of us trying to get Him to do what we want or trying to subdue people by us becoming the covering.

This horse has the covering of holiness and Christ is the rider. He makes war in righteousness.

> 12. *And his eyes were as a flame of fire, and on his head were many crowns; and he had a name written, that no one has known, but he himself.*

> 13. *And he was clothed with a garment dipped in blood; and his name is called The Word of God.*

Without the application of the blood, there is no covering. Furthermore, the blood is applied with hyssop, and hyssop is the symbol of humility (Exodus 12:22). The Lord must deal with our arrogance, with our pride, and with our dominance in order to apply the blood. The result of applying the blood is that we will be clothed in the righteousness of Christ under the covering of the Holy Spirit; we are to be under the government of Christ. Now Christ is seated over us (upon the white horse) instead of us trying to ride Him. This is the difference between the covering of man and the covering of God.

Under the covering of God, He will use us in many ways but in different manners. The one who will be greatest in the kingdom of the heavens is the one who is the servant of all.

> 14. *And the armies that are in the heaven followed him upon white horses, clothed in fine linen, white and clean.*

> 15. *And out of his mouth goes a sharp sword, that with it he should smite the Gentiles; and he shall rule them with a rod of iron; and he treads the winepress of the fierceness and wrath of Almighty God.*

> 16. *And he has on his garment and on his thigh a name written, KING OF KINGS, AND LORD OF LORDS.*

But this communion cup, this blood that must be applied, is death to the old man, and in the same manner is life to the new man. He who drinks this cup unworthily is drinking condemnation, but he who does this after having had an encounter and a covenant with God at the altar of God will receive sustenance and life. This person will begin to participate in the life of the Lord (Romans 5:10).

> *The love of God is not born out of sentiments; it is born of sacrifice.*

In Revelation 6:9, the souls of the redeemed are found under the altar. This means that they are protected (covered) because they are in covenant with God and nothing can touch them. The Lord is waiting for the moment of the resurrection to put His government on display in a visible manner. Therefore, if we do not understand about the altar, if we do not understand about the cross, it is not possible to understand the gospel, and it is not possible to receive the covering of the Spirit of God.

After a person has received the covering of the Spirit of God, nothing and no one can touch them. The apostle Paul says that after this, *We are confident, I say, and willing rather to be absent from the body and present with the Lord* (2 Corinthians 5:1-11). For the person who has entered the way of the cross by the altar of God, for the person who has experienced the fire of God, for the person who has received the Spirit of God, the things of this world are no longer important. Their values have changed and their desires have changed. This person remains lit on fire with the true fire of God, which is the love of God that redeems. The love of God is not born out of sentiments; it is born of sacrifice.

Let us pray

> *Lord, we ask that this message remain clear, and that your altar, the way of the cross, will be restored anew in the Church. May there be new ministers of your altar who will conduct the people into a true encounter with the fire of God. May the power of sin and of guilt be broken before covenants done your way, Lord. May the gospel of the kingdom of God be restored in the Church. May we witness and experience the conversions and changed lives of persons who, like Paul, will leave everything behind and not pay any more attention to the things of this world, but that they may fix their eyes on the goal of perfection. We ask this in the name of our Lord Jesus. Amen.*

Note

This was the second message preached in Colombia using what is now known as the Spanish *Reina Valera 2000* or *Sagradas Escrituras Version Antigua* (*Jubilee Bible 2000* in English). The message was given in the early spring of the year 2000 and set the foundation for multiplication of ministry and outreach all over Colombia and into other countries. I had just finished spending almost ten years working on these two Bibles.

The Altar and the Blood was published in 2009 in Spanish as the first message in a book of eleven messages entitled *The Altar and the Gospel.* We estimate that this message alone may have aired over a thousand times on radio stations all over Colombia and elsewhere and on the Internet. It is also interesting to note that we now have compiled close to a thousand messages of this quality as we preach through the Bible.

The messages that we are producing in this place (in Colombia to be broadcast into the war zone) are being preached using

Las Sagradas Escrituras Version Antigua (*Jubilee Bible 2000* in English) published by Colombia Para Cristo, Bogota, Colombia. The first thing someone asked me on the two or three occasions I had shown him the Bible was, "Brother, how much does a copy of this Bible cost?"

The first reply that I gave was, "I think it costs about ten thousand pesos [about $5.00 US]." However, I soon began to think differently. How much does it cost? Almost all of those who were used by God to write portions of this book paid with their lives. The central person of history and of the Scriptures, the Lord Jesus, gave His life for us.

The altar in the Old Testament is comparable to the cross in the New Testament. All through history, the apostles who wrote bits and pieces of the Scriptures gave their lives so we could have this. The early church and those who remained faithful after them tried to protect the written Word against loss and contamination.

Consider the Waldenses, who lived beside Switzerland in the mountains of Europe and who gave up almost a million martyrs. The main thing that cost so many lives was that they refused to give up their Bible manuscripts to the agents of the Inquisition.

We could go on with the story. The early Reformation translation of the NT was done by the one who started the Spanish Bible, a man named Francisco de Encinas. He thought that if he could only get a copy of the New Testament to the king of Spain, and he'd receive and distribute it, things could change in Spain.

He went to the palace with the first New Testament (published in 1543) dedicated to the king and managed to get inside and deliver it, but the agents of the Inquisition captured him and put him in jail. After a miracle of God, the Lord got him out of the prison. In the end, no one knows what happened to him; some say they killed him, others say not.

Another man, Juan Pineda, translated the Psalms and added them to the New Testament of Francisco de Encinas. He was also terribly persecuted and paid a great price.

Casiodoro de Reina began to read the Hebrew Bible that was in his monastery chained to a post as a relic. (They were told to touch it and kiss it but not to read it!) He began to read and translate the Old Testament and explain the real message of the altar, and the monks were converted. The Inquisition came to kill all of them but at least two managed to escape (Casiodoro de Reina and Cipriano de Valera and possibly some others).

William Tyndale, who did the first English translation that was printed, was forced to flee his home. They persecuted him. A criminal won his confidence and helped him smuggle Bibles into England but betrayed him in the end. William Tyndale was strangled and burned at the stake.

The Jubilee Bible has been compared with the work of each of these men, and each has contributed greatly. Modern translations have minimized (translating in a very different manner) and sometimes even discarded the portions that these men considered to be crucial. Words like *judgment, repentance, holiness* and even the word *blood* have been whittled away little by little, because the devil knows that if he can do away with the altar, there will be nothing left.

Russell M. Stendal

June 7, 2013

CHAPTER 3

The System of Leviathan

In the year 2000, when I finished editing the Jubilee Bible, the last book that I checked was the book of Job. This was the book that the Lord had me preach from at the funeral for the wife of Brother Clayt Sonmore, Sister Jean. This chapter is a reflection on the book of Job.

Many times we do not understand why people who have communion with the Lord go through major (and sometimes even long-term) difficulties. In the previous chapter about the altar and the blood, the altar symbolizes the conditions of the gospel; it symbolizes making a covenant with God His way. Furthermore, when we present ourselves to the Lord as a living sacrifice, from that point on we do not belong to ourselves; we belong to God.

This is how the book of Job begins, where we see Job offering burnt offerings (holocausts) and sacrifices to God for his children. Job was already in covenant with God. In the original texts, the word holocaust is used in Scripture in reference to Jacob's ladder and means "to ascend." This word symbolizes an open path between heaven and earth. The person who enters into a covenant with God and participates in this holocaust has an open heaven.

Another use of this word holocaust occurs when the angel of God spoke with the parents of Samson. Knowing that God was going to use him to begin to deliver his people, he gave them instructions about how to raise their child. In this context, Samson's father Manoah asked the angel to reveal his name so that Manoah and his wife might honor him when his word was fulfilled.

> And the angel of the LORD replied, Why dost thou ask
> for my name? It is wonderful (Judges 13:18).

Further on it says that the angel did wondrously, because when they offered the burnt offering (holocaust) to the Lord and *the flame went up toward heaven from off the altar, that the angel of the LORD ascended in the flame of the altar as Manoah and his wife looked on* (Judges 13:20).

The holocaust of a true covenant with the Lord opens heaven. It opens the possibility that we may participate in the nature of God, and it also opens the possibility for us to have direct communion with God, where not only does He hear us, but we also hear Him. Job lived like this in covenant with God.

When the enemy (Satan) came and told God, *Does Job fear God for nothing? Hast thou not made a hedge about him and about his house and about all that he has on every side? Thou hast blessed the work of his hands; therefore, his substance has increased in the land. But put forth thy hand now and touch all that he has, and thou shalt see if he will not blaspheme thee to thy face* (Job 1:9-11), the Lord gave Satan permission to go after Job, but he did not blaspheme the name of God like Satan wanted.

The Lord put Job into Satan's hands with the only condition that Job's life be preserved. Job was unable to understand what had happened, and to make matters worse, three friends showed up to comfort him. Thinking they were helping him, these supposed comforters began to lay a guilt trip on Job.

All of the names of Job's friends are symbolic, but we will only make reference to the first of the three, Eliphaz the Temanite. This name alludes to the soft, warm wind that blows from the south. Eliphaz symbolizes those who preach a gospel that tells the people that when they come to the Lord, everything will get better. "If you receive the Lord, He will give you health and prosperity and anything you desire. If any of this is lacking, it is surely because you have hidden sin in your life."

Eliphaz had two other friends whose names also symbolize errors in the religious system. They symbolize when people fall into one of two errors – the error of legalism, trying to apply the principles and the law of God according to our own wisdom, and the error of licentiousness, thinking that everyone can do as they please because they are protected in advance by the Lord. These errors have remained in the people of the Lord from the beginning and, as with all corruption, are getting worse.

The Spirit of God may work through us and may use many and different people.

After much dialogue between Job and his three friends, the three men quit talking because it was impossible for them to answer Job who insisted on declaring himself righteous.

Job 32

1. *So these three men ceased to answer Job because he was righteous in his own eyes.*

They were unable to answer Job based on their application of the Law and the principles of God. However, a young man named Elihu did speak on behalf of the Spirit of God.

All through the Scriptures, there are people who represent the Spirit of God, but in none of these cases can we affirm that these people are the Spirit of God. The Spirit of God may work through us and may use many and different people.

In the case of the prophet Balaam, there was only a don-key, and the Spirit of God used it to say what needed to be said at the moment (Numbers 22:30). In some of the books of the Bible, we are tempted to say that a person represents God, yet this is certain only when God is speaking or acting through this person. For example: Someone can say something edify-ing and anointed in a meeting that is being directed by God, but if we are not careful, five minutes later the same person can say something on their own that contradicts everything. Peter could say, *Thou art the Christ*, and a few verses later he rebuked the Lord for explaining to them how He was going to be crucified. Jesus had to tell Peter, *Remove thyself from before me, Satan* (Matthew 16:23).

We must be careful with these identifications. In the case of Job, the Spirit of God used Elihu and showed many things through him. When the Spirit of God is in us, the Lord can use us to give a word or to receive a word. The Lord began to answer Job through Elihu (after Job had been complaining that God would not stand up like a man and answer him), and in one verse Elihu says, *for I yet speak on God's behalf* (Job 36:2).

On many occasions, I have had to give an answer from God to someone. One time the commander of an armed group said to me, "I have been observing you and your brother for many years, and I see that you are in communion with God and that you hear the voice of God." After a bit he continued, "I want to know how I can hear the voice of God."

So I answered him, "If you want to hear from God, I am here representing Him, and the message that I have from God to you is that all of us, sooner or later, will have to answer for our deeds before God. I must answer for mine; you will answer for yours. This is what God is saying to you now. But if you desire to hear the voice of God on your own in an intimate way, it is necessary to have a clean heart; this is the requirement."

We must come before the Lord in repentance and suffer the entire process of the altar. A complete surrender of our sin, our guilt, and ourselves will open the heavens, and we will enter in to have intimate and direct communion with the Lord. I spent about an hour answering his question.

Without going over all that Elihu said, a few lines stand out:

Job 33

23. *If there is a messenger with him, an interpreter, one among a thousand, to show unto man his uprightness;*

24. *to tell him that God had mercy on him, that he delivered him from going down to the pit; that he found a ransom;*

The Lord is that ransom for us. The covering mentioned in the previous chapter is the ransom that the Lord Jesus paid for us by His blood. It is through this ransom, through this blood that we can have the covering of the Spirit of God. The following verses sum up the problem. In Job 34, it says:

5. *For Job has said, I am righteous; and God has taken away my right.*

Job had still not understood some things about his covenant with God. When we enter into a covenant with God and are no longer our own, we have been bought by the Lord with a great price; we belong to Him (1 Corinthians 6:20). The Lord can do what He pleases with us. This was the difficult part for Job to understand. And if it was difficult for Job to understand this, imagine the problem trying to get this across to his three friends! In Job 37, Elihu explained why the Lord allows difficulties in life. The difficulties are represented by the cold or by ice or by the wind. In the Bibles of the early Reformation, the cold north wind is called "Aquilon." This kills and wipes out everything that is green. Why does the Lord allow seasons like this in our lives?

Eliphaz the Temanite only understood when the warm south wind blew. This wind brought the springtime and made all the trees bud and bloom. It caused the fruit to come forth and indicated when it was time to plant, to harvest, to reap a bounty – the time for prosperity. But Elihu explained why the north wind comes bringing difficulties.

Job 37

9. *Out of the south comes the whirlwind and cold out of the north wind.*

10. *By the breath of God ice is given; and the broad waters are constrained.*

11. *In addition to this, with clarity he wearies the thick clouds; and he scatters them with his light.*

12. *And they are turned round about by his counsels; that they may do whatever he commands them upon the face of the world in the earth.*

13. *On some occasions for correction, on others for his land, on others for mercy he causes them to appear.*

These clouds of judgment that He wearies or scatters with His light, He places on some occasions for correction, on others for His land (His people), and on others for mercy. He causes them to appear. This is why the Lord allows difficulties in the life of the believer. Eliphaz and his two friends thought that adversity was correction that came only because someone did something bad. Elihu understood that there are two more reasons:

1. **Because of His land** (His land is His people). We are in a great battle, and God is raising up a people according to His design so they might receive the fullness of the inheritance; therefore, He must form them, discipline them, teach them. There is an enemy who is against the land of God, who is the accuser of the brethren, and this enemy must be vanquished. The enemy can only be defeated if things are done God's way. So Elihu prepared the way for what God would teach directly to Job.

2. **For mercy**. God extends mercy over His people, even if it does not seem that way at the time.

One of the things that the Lord was emphasizing to us with Brother Clayt Sonmore, his wife Jean, and to everyone else is that through all these difficulties, Job was able to say at the end (after he repented before the Lord for his bad attitude in telling God that He had taken away his rights) that up until then, he had only been able to hear, but now he could see; therefore, he repented in dust and ashes. The entire

> *God extends mercy over His people, even if it does not seem that way at the time.*

trajectory of difficulties that happened in the life of Job served the purpose of translating him from the realm of only hearing to the realm of being able to see God.

There is a realm of being able to see God or to see things from God's point of view. It is not possible to be in this realm without passing through trials and tribulations. We must pass through the trial to see if our goals are the things of this world or if our goal is the kingdom of God and the things of His invisible realm. Without the test, it is not possible to know; it is not possible to see clearly.

After Elihu explained these things to Job, he was able to offer some comfort. The other comforters were unable to console Job, but Elihu could.

Job 37

14. Hearken unto this, Job; stand still, and consider the wondrous works of God.

Yes, there will be an answer! Calm down, Job, and God will answer you.

24. Men, therefore, shall fear him; all the crafty of heart shall not see him.

Those who are crafty of heart and seek to get things on their own will never see God nor be able to see things as they are. For those who are crafty, to enter the presence of God would be their destruction; they would never be able to stand in the presence of God.

After this, the Lord answered Job and began to ask him questions. Job had been insisting on presenting his case before the Lord and having God declare him righteous. Even though the Lord did do this at the end – for He declared that Job had spoken by Him in uprightness – He also taught Job some very important things. He taught Job that even though he was righteous before, during, and after the problem, Job was not more righteous than God. So in chapter 40 Job says:

4. Behold, I am vile; what shall I answer thee? I will lay my hand over my mouth.

5. Once I have spoken; but I will not answer; even twice, but I will proceed no further.

Note the sequence. Job spoke with his three friends until they were unable to answer. Elihu, by the Spirit of God, presented arguments to Job that he could not answer. Then God spoke directly to Job, and when the Lord had obtained the right attitude in Job (where Job rested his case and did not ask for any more explanations from God about what was happening), He began to open Job's eyes so he could see the situation from God's perspective. It is in this moment that God opened Job's eyes to see how things really are.

Now Job could see that this was not just a situation involving individuals who were treated justly or unjustly. This was a much larger battle. This was a problem of such magnitude that no man could solve it.

The only one who can manage these situations is God. He does this so that we may come out of this into freedom, so that the entire creation can be freed from the fall. It is absolutely necessary to learn to do things God's way. This will lead us to the way of the cross. The way of God leads to the altar.

15. *Behold now behemoth, which I made with thee;*
he eats grass as an ox.

With this, the Lord is speaking of all the natural creation. The Lord created us in Adam, and in Adam we all fell. All creation fell. Grass is symbolic of the food for the natural, fallen man who is like a beast.

16. *Behold now, his strength is in his loins, and his*
force is in the navel of his belly.

Natural appetites manage all of the natural creation. All the animals have to be continually searching for food; this is their life day after day. The life of the natural man is to seek his daily bread without rest for the duration of his life. He must be seeking his own things. The symbol of his life is his navel (his navel symbolizes his carnal appetites).

An old fable in the north told about a certain character who had to choose between seven little old men who were almost identical. If he could pick Adam out of the group, he would go to heaven; otherwise, he would go to hell. He made the right choice, and when someone asked him how he did it, he replied, "It was easy. I picked the one with no belly button!" Even though we do not know exactly where this fable came from, we do know that Adam was created in an environment where he was not a slave to his natural appetites and carnal desires. Adam was in the garden to dress it and keep it. He could eat freely of the fruit of all the trees in the garden (except one) and had access to all the provision of God. His sustenance was his communion with God. But after the fall, he had to live by the sweat of his brow. And we do know that after Adam, all of us were born with a navel; we are born into the realm of the belly and controlled by its appetites.

17. *He moves his tail like a cedar; the sinews of his stones are wrapped together.*

The natural creation is locked in genetically with no natural way out. Not only does it reproduce according to its species, according to its genre, and according to its nature (this is what the old manuscripts of the Bible literally say), but also from generation to generation it is degenerating more and more. As time goes on, more defects, more problems, and more diseases appear because everything in the natural realm is degenerating due to corruption. On the other hand, in the way and order of the new creation, everything is ascending along the way of redemption and restoration.

18. *His bones are as strong as brass; his members are like bars of iron.*

Brass is a symbol of judgment (and sin). Iron is a symbol of the law (and control), and the only way to control this natural creation is with law. And the *law of sin and death* is built right into him.

19. *He is the beginning of the ways of God; he that made him shall make his sword draw near unto him.*

This is very interesting to note because the natural creation is the beginning of the ways of God. God uses the natural creation to plant the new creation. We have our beginning in Adam (in the old creation), but we have the opportunity to be able to receive the Word of God (the sword which will circumcise the heart and cut the control of the flesh). We have the opportunity to receive an incorruptible seed, and God can continue His creation process until He is able to take us out of the old creation and place us into Christ in the new creation, until we can say, *old things are passed away; behold, all things are made new* (2 Corinthians 5:17). This is God's plan for each one of us. It is not like we have to say in many groups and churches if we are really honest: "A few little things passed away, and some other little things are new." We can say it only this way because many times a corruptible seed is being planted instead of an incorruptible seed.

> *The natural man is always seeking a way out and thinks that he can overcome death.*

20. *Surely the mountains bring him forth food, where all the beasts of the field play.*

21. *He shall lie down under the shade, in the covert of the reeds and of the damp places.*

He always seeks his own comfort. He is looking for covering and comfort.

22. *The shady trees cover him with their shadow; the willows of the brook compass him about.*

23. *Behold, he shall drink up a river and not change; he trusts that he can draw up the Jordan into his mouth.*

The natural man is always seeking a way out and thinks that he can overcome death. He thinks he can live his life according to his whims and that even the Jordan of death will not faze him. He thinks he can drink up the Jordan (symbol of death) and get away with it. Look, however, at what comes next:

24. *His maker shall take him by the weakness of his eyes in a snare, and pierce through his nose.*

Why? Because the natural man wants to have everything he sees. This same desire will cause him to fall into God's trap. Then God will be able to get control, dominate him, tame him, and manage him. The natural man and the natural creation are not the main problem; God can manage them. Our fight is not with flesh and blood; it is with powers of wickedness in high places. This is what God showed Job (Ephesians 6:12).

Job 41

1. *Canst thou draw out leviathan with a hook or with the cord which thou lettest down on his tongue?*

Now God is speaking of spiritual powers and is naming the strongest of them, which appears here with the name Leviathan. The description is that of a dragon. He is represented from the beginning as the ancient serpent and in the book of Revelation as the dragon (Revelation 12:9).

2. *Canst thou put a hook into his nose or bore his jaw through with a thorn?*

3. *Will he make many supplications unto thee? Will he speak soft words unto thee?*

4. *Will he make a covenant with thee that thou shall take him for a slave for ever?*

5. *Wilt thou play with him as with a bird?*

6. Shall the companions make a banquet of him? Shall they part him among the merchants?

7. Canst thou cut his skin with knives or his head with a fish spear?

8. Lay thine hand upon him; thou shalt remember the battle and do no more.

This is what the church has not understood in Pentecost. They have thought that with the gifts of God, with the gifts that we have received from Him, we can go out on our own and trap the enemy. Not so. This enemy cannot be overcome in this manner. There is only one way to overcome him, which we will explain later. Nevertheless, this is not the tactic that the organized church has been practicing, and this is why they have not been able to overcome him. This is why the problem is getting worse. Notice that God is revealing how this enemy is to Job and is directly uncovering the problem.

9. Behold, your hope regarding him shall fail; for even at the sight of him they shall faint.

We have had many friends who were willing to fight this enemy, and when they engaged the battle they were unable to stand. Others were too afraid to even attempt to stand.

10. No one is so bold as to dare stir him up; who then shall be able to stand before me?

It has been said that Leviathan is very terrible and no one can stand against him. So God is saying that if no one can stand against him, "Who can stand against me?" This is an interesting twist, and the Lord is going to show that this will be very important to consider. What if we are found on the wrong side of the fence?

11. *Who has preceded me, that I should repay him?*
All that is under the whole heaven is mine.

Leviathan was not first. God existed before Leviathan. God does not owe anything to Leviathan. God is the only one who can handle him. No one can serve two masters (Matthew 6:24). We will either be found pushing back against Leviathan even if it costs us our life or else we will be found grieving the Holy Spirit and pushing back against God in order to please Leviathan.

Verse 12 of chapter 41 has been mistranslated in almost every Bible. Checking the words and translating this according to the way the same word is translated everywhere else gives the following rendition of verse 12:

12. *I will not conceal his lies, nor his might, nor the*
beauty of his order.

Leviathan was a murderer from the beginning, a liar and the father of lies (John 8:44). Without any provocation, he presented himself before Eve with the purpose of deceiving her, and he did this with lies. God had said one thing, and Leviathan replied that it was really some other way, changing the word of the Lord for lies. Why? Because God was giving a lot of power and authority to Adam and Eve, and maybe Leviathan felt that if he did not take them out, he would end up under their dominion. He wanted to be the one to dominate everyone.

Scripture clearly states that the reason for his fall was that he attempted to exalt his throne (Isaiah 14). When he attempted this, evil was found in him. It was not sufficient for him to deceive Eve and cause Adam to sin, resulting in their being cast out of the garden. Later, as God prophesied that the seed of the woman would crush his head, he decided to kill Abel by using his brother Cain in an attempt to wipe out this seed. But he has not accomplished all of his plans, even though he has restricted the church and, in most cases, dominated the people of God. He is the god of this world and he has a lot of power in the realm of this world. This verse speaks of his lies, his might, and his order, the order of Leviathan.

When I searched for the roots and trajectory of the word Leviathan, I thought that it would be snake, serpent, dragon, worm, or something along these lines. But Leviathan comes from the word Levi. The root of the word Leviathan is located in Genesis 29. This is concerning Leah, the wife of Jacob.

> 34. *And she conceived again and gave birth to a son; and said, Now this time will my husband be joined unto me because I have born him three sons; therefore his name was called Levi.*

The word *joined* (union or united) is the root of the word Levi and also of the word Leviathan.

This is the desire of human beings, to be joined one to another and seek a union. This was the problem at the tower of Babel. They wanted to unite and make a tower unto heaven.

Right now, Leviathan is running a great many Christian groups.

The word Levi runs its course throughout the Bible, and in the Old Testament, this word ends in the book of the prophet Zechariah where it says, *many ... shall join themselves unto the LORD in that day.* The union that God is looking for is union with Him. If we are joined to Him in covenant with Him, with a full surrender to Him, and by the application of the blood at the altar (after being sealed and covered by the Spirit of God), He will automatically put us in harmony with everyone else who has the same purpose, the same covenant, the same covering, and the same head. But when man opens up a forced unity where he desires control, then the system of Leviathan dominates. Right now, Leviathan is running a great many Christian groups. Leviathan is the system of this world. It runs the governments of this world.

Let's take a look at this system of Leviathan. What is *the beauty of his order*? When things go wrong here on earth, it seems good to have someone in charge to resolve the issues. Israel had the same problem. They wanted a king like all the other nations. They wanted someone visible who would give them orders and settle their problems. On that occasion, this is what the Lord said to Samuel:

> *Hearken unto the voice of the people in all that they say unto thee, for they have not rejected thee, but they have rejected me that I should not reign over them* (1 Samuel 8:7).

In the order of the Lord, He is the head and no one can harm Him or replace Him. At the present time, eastern Colombia has many problems including persecution of the churches with the heads of these churches fleeing. The congregation of the Lord (Greek "ekklesia" or "called-out ones") does not have a head here on the earth; the head is in heaven and no one can harm Him. Only in the order of Leviathan are there heads here on earth. In the book of Revelation, the system of Leviathan is described as a dragon with seven heads (symbolic of many heads). Actually, there are heads all over the place. Right now, there are over two thousand major religious heads all over the world, each with their own doctrine.

Zechariah 14

9. *And the LORD shall be king over all the earth; in that day the LORD shall be one, and his name one.*

The Lord Jesus repeated this same concept when He said *there shall be one fold and one shepherd* (John 10:16), and it is very clear that He is that Shepherd (or Pastor).

Scripture speaks of the beauty of the order of Leviathan. This is a dragon, according to his description, that has scales that are ordered, and this appears beautiful in our sight. To those who are still operating in the order and nature of Adam, the order of Leviathan appears perfect; it seems to be the way to foster the church.

Job 41

13. *Who shall uncover the face of his garment? Or who shall come to him with a double bridle?*

Who can control this system? We cannot control this system. The system will control us! Who can uncover and reveal the interior of the order of Leviathan and make this known? If someone begins to tell the people who are under a government or a religious organization that this is not of God, they will be rejected. Who can open up this covering that they have and expose what is really inside? Whoever desires to expose the system has to be willing to pay with their very life and reputation or they will be unable to uncover it.

14. *Who shall open the doors of his face? The orders of his teeth are terrible.*

Whoever opens *the doors of his face* will encounter ordered rows of razor-sharp teeth ready to devour. These teeth are also revealed to whoever does not desire to walk according to their order. Whoever begins to expose the doors of the face of Leviathan must be willing to pay with their lives (or at least with their reputations). Many of those who have done this over the centuries have paid with their lives.

15. *His scales* [Hebrew "shields"] *are his pride, shut up together as with a close seal.*

The seal of the order of Leviathan is always his pride. This arrogance and pride are so strong that the ruling class will put down anyone who confronts them, because they claim to be the only ones who know how to make things function. They think that because they are the only ones who know, they have this great knowledge and they have this profound understanding of tremendous and intimate things so no one else can tell them anything. The people who subscribe to the system and attain a position of command become part of a superior class that is above everyone else. The rest of the people belong to a lower class, and those in this class do not have the right to question any of the actions of the ruling class because, according to the insiders, these people know nothing.

16. *One is so near to another, that no air can come between them.*

So this seal, this mark of Leviathan, are some scales (or shields) of pride so jammed together and so intertwined one with another that the air (the same word in Hebrew as "spirit") cannot penetrate. This pride, this arrogance that protects and covers this system is so closed that the Spirit cannot enter. They function with another spirit. It is a spirit that manipulates the people with feelings of guilt. Whoever did not pay their tithe, whoever did not attend mass, whoever did not go to the church service on Sunday, whoever did not do whatever thing that the ruling class required is induced into tremendous feelings of guilt. So the person begins to think that they should repent and do whatever is being required. One is so near to another that the wind or breath of the Spirit cannot come between them.

This same spirit permeates the secular realm and bombards anyone who does not blindly obey the rules and regulations of Leviathan with guilt and shame. Anyone who will appease

Leviathan by being politically correct must therefore go against their conscience and grieve the Holy Spirit.

> 17. *They are joined one to another; they stick together, that they cannot be separated.*

This is the description of Leviathan. This is a perversion of Levi and of the true and healthy bond in the Spirit that joins the true body of Christ. Those of the body of Christ are all brothers and are all servants. There is only one class: the priesthood of all believers.

> *The people who subscribe to the system and attain a position of command become part of a superior class that is above everyone else.*

> 18. *By his sneezings lights are lit, and his eyes are like the eyelids of the morning.*

> 19. *Out of his mouth go burning lamps, and sparks of fire leap out.*

> 20. *Out of his nostrils goes forth smoke, as out of a seething pot or caldron.*

> 21. *His breath kindles coals, and a flame goes out of his mouth.*

This system has its own fire. It is not the fire of God. Wherever it permeates, it generates a fire that appears supernatural (and in many cases it is) except that it is not the true fire of God. *His eyes are like the eyelids of the morning*, always promising a new day that they are unable to deliver and always promising to deliver the people. Everything they do has a supernatural element to it. From the days of the golden calf, this type of false fire has been prevalent. What explanation did Aaron, the son of Levi, give regarding the fire and the golden calf? He said:

And I answered unto them, Whoever has any gold,
let them break it off. So they gave it to me and I cast
it into the fire, and this calf came out (Exodus 32:24).

We cast in the gold and this calf came out, so what could we do but worship it? A miracle! All those who are intertwined forming the system of Leviathan, the perverted Levitical priesthood that promotes and provides horizontal union without linking each member with the true head in heaven, foment their order with false fire. They foster their own business with the false fire by saying, "There were miracles, and therefore we are justified."

For the orthodox from the tomb of Jesus, a fire comes forth and illuminates the three crosses that they have in Jerusalem. And for each one of the images in the Catholic Church, there is a "miraculous" history. They do not say who made it, how much it cost, or how it was contracted. There is always a story about the statue of a virgin that simply appeared somewhere or about someone who came down from heaven. There is always a miraculous story about the procedure. Now, in the charismatic realm, there are prophets who run around putting together the same kind of horizontal union, fomenting the same system.

Remember the parable of the wheat and the tares? Remember that the tares are gathered first in bundles (to be burned) and then the wheat is harvested? Those who are bundling the tares are even now gathering and joining everyone whom they can convince with false fire. There are people interceding and prophesying, but who cares if they bark like dogs or slither like serpents, creating a tremendous spectacle and an apparent supernatural anointing. This dragon is a fire dragon, but it is not the fire of God; it is false fire.

22. *In his neck dwells strength, and before him the*
work is undone.

God told Israel that they were a stiff-necked people, and the neck of Leviathan is very strong. Here is the secret of his strength because he will not bow before the Lord. He wants everyone to bow before him!

The true work of the Lord cannot be accomplished by the system of Leviathan. The system of Leviathan can communicate the love of man but not the love of God. The love of God is very different. The love of God is born of sacrifice and redeems by its very nature. Human love is a sentiment that can produce a horizontal union, but without the love of God, this only serves to tighten the scales of Leviathan. This makes it virtually impossible for the person to be led by the Spirit of God because they always have to be in accord with everyone else and with the hierarchy in order to do anything. This virtually ensures that there will always be at least several in the mix with the spirit of Leviathan. Secular and religious governments, multinational firms: virtually any entity run by committee is susceptible to the spirit of Leviathan. God places responsibility upon individuals (not committees).

The next verse in Job 41 has been mistranslated in almost every Bible. Notice what it literally says:

> 23. *The failings of his flesh are joined together; his flesh is firm in him and does not move.*

Leviathan cannot overcome the flesh. The flesh is the firmness of his being, because without it there would be no feelings of guilt. Without feelings of guilt, it is not possible to manage his system. Anyone in the system of Leviathan will find it difficult if not impossible to overcome the flesh. The failings of the flesh are there; they are part of the system. Those who are part of the system of Leviathan, especially the leaders, always justify *the failings of his flesh.*

Since the leaders walk in pedophilia, adultery, homosexuality, and in every type of sin, they turn this around and say that if God can forgive them, He can forgive anyone any time, any place, and for anything. They are preaching the love of man as if God were like us. This is to recreate a god in our own fallen image instead of us being redeemed and conformed to His image. Totally inverted. They can never get out from under the failings of the flesh. The only thing they can do is cover their problems with the shields of pride and the arrogance that comes from their extensive human knowledge.

> *They are preaching the love of man as if God were like us.*

24. *His heart is as firm as a stone; as hard as a piece of the lower millstone.*

This verse shows a very great truth; in reality, this system does not have a heart for the people. The people are not important; what is important is to strengthen and increase the system. Individuals (who might have a heart for God and for other individuals) are not allowed to make spontaneous decisions on their own in direct and immediate response to the Spirit of God. Everyone is subject to group think and the system.

25. *Of his greatness, the mighty are afraid; by reason of breakings they remove sin from themselves.*

In the system of Leviathan, leaders try to get rid of sin by using terror tactics in the realm of blind submission to their rules and regulations. In the religious realm they have the people fast, pray, do penance, tithe, go to services, and attend unending religious rituals, but they cannot eliminate sin. They are always looking to see if someone has a problem so they can accuse them. Fear and force are their preferred tools. On the other hand, God dominates sin in a different manner. The Lord wants us to enter into His nature. He wants to change us from the inside out. His entry into our being will cost us our own autonomy, yet in Matthew 11 it says:

> 30. *For my yoke is easy, and my burden is light.*

In the system of Leviathan, the yoke is hard and the burden is heavy. The leaders keep heaping on more and more load and are unable to give the slightest help in lifting it. They say, "Don't do this, don't do that," and on and on and on.

> 26. *When one catches up to him, no sword or spear or dart or coat of mail shall endure against him.*

> 27. *He esteems iron as straw and bronze as rotten wood.*

> 28. *The arrow cannot make him flee; with him, sling-stones are turned into stubble.*

> 29. *He counts any weapon as stubble; he laughs at the shaking of the spear.*

If we attack him, it will not work. Everything imaginable has been tried and he sneers at all of it. Even the giant, Goliath, could be brought down by a well-placed sling stone. David then cut his head off with a sword and went all the way to Jerusalem showing off the giant's head (see 1 Samuel 17:54), but what happened next? Saul got jealous of him and marked him and did not let up until he had driven David out of the land as a fugitive. To combat the system of Leviathan, we need another procedure. The gifts that we have, the weapons that we have, are not working. Not even the sword works against Leviathan.

> 30. *Broken clay vessels are under him; he carves his imprint upon the mire.*

Leviathan is under a curse and has to crawl on his belly (Genesis 3:14). God binds him to the realm of natural desires. His pastime is to break clay vessels. What are we in the hands of the Lord? Clay vessels. What does Leviathan like to do? He likes to break clay vessels and carve his imprint upon the mire, upon humanity. He desires to imprint his mark, the mark of the beast (which is primarily a way of thinking and acting). This is what he does all over the place. The only way out of this is a complete surrender to the Lord and receiving His seal. The mark that represents Him is the Holy Spirit. This is the covering.

31. *He makes the deep to boil like a pot; he makes the sea like a pot of ointment.*

Leviathan has a false anointing.

32. *He makes the path shine after him; one would think the deep to be hoary.*

Oil rises to the surface of the water, and wherever Leviathan goes, he leaves a trail and a false anointing that appears to calm the waters. His ministers appear to be ministers of light. A counterfeiter will not try to make false twenty-five-dollar bills or false thirty-dollar bills; he will make the counterfeit money appear as close to the real thing as possible. The enemy is trying to do things as close to how God is doing them as possible. However, the enemy cannot deliver anyone from the power of the flesh. He cannot produce the anointing that destroys the yoke (Isaiah 10:27). He cannot produce the fruit of righteousness. He can only produce a kingdom of fear and terror where no one is at peace and everyone is plagued by feelings of guilt.

The individuals and agencies under his command do not trust one another. There is continual warfare within the system of Leviathan. Jesus said that a kingdom divided against itself cannot stand (Matthew 12:25,26).

33. *Upon earth there is not his like, who behaves without fear.*

The earth in Scripture is symbolic of the inheritance of God, the true church. Leviathan thinks that he can wreak havoc in the world and in the church with complete impunity.

> 34. *He despises all exalted things; he is king over all the sons of pride.*

This is Leviathan. The only way to take him down, the only thing that he does not understand is something called the way of the cross.

Instead of taking our spiritual gifts and launching a war against him, the Lord wants to mold us into a weapon in His hands. In Isaiah 27, the Lord says that He will deal with Leviathan.

> 1. *In that day the LORD with his sore and great and strong sword shall visit punishment upon leviathan the fleeing serpent, and upon leviathan that serpent of double vision; and he shall slay the dragon that is in the sea.*

The only way to overcome him is for the Lord to do it. And how is the Lord going to accomplish this? The Lord has a body here on the earth which is part of Himself. This body has entered into Him and because of this, the members have received the Spirit of God. They do not go forth with their gifts seeking personal gain. They go forth in the way of the cross, willing to lay down their lives to do the will of God.

This is the theme of Hebrews 11 that speaks of the heroes of the faith, and this theme runs throughout the Bible. Even Samson with all his gifts and errors accomplished more through his death than through his life. This is what the Lord explained to Job. Job wanted to know why the Lord would permit the devil to take hold of him in such a fashion. The Lord explained that it was because Job symbolized the Lord Jesus Christ and all the body of Christ.

The Lord overcame the devil on the cross. When the devil thought he was killing the Son of God, he was really doing himself in. Scripture says that in every matter there must be two or three witnesses. According to the Word, a charge cannot even be leveled against an elder in the church if there are not two or three witnesses. The Lord is one witness. But in order to completely sink the devil, two or three witnesses are necessary. Where are we going to get them? There must be a remnant, a people who will follow the steps of the Lord. There must be a clean bride without spot or wrinkle or any such thing as the second witness. In the book of Revelation, two witnesses appear.

> *And the Spirit and the bride say, Come. And let him*
> *that hears say, Come. And let him that is thirsty come;*
> *and whosoever will, let him take of the water of life,*
> *freely* (Revelation 22:17).

Here are two witnesses, two testimonies each saying the same thing. This is not what we have had throughout history. We have had the Spirit saying one thing and the bride here on the earth saying another thing. There have not been two witnesses. This is why the Lord showed Job the only way to overcome Leviathan, the order of Leviathan, and the devil and his system. Leviathan represents more than just the devil. It is an entire secular and religious order that no one can touch. Without taking down Leviathan (and without freeing those trapped in Leviathan), there cannot be a clean bride here on the earth; there must be one or the other (see Revelation 17). There cannot be two entities at the same time both claiming to be the bride. Is it the clean woman or is it the other woman who is riding the beast, drinking abominations from a cup filled with blood? It's one or the other.

Job 42

1. *Then Job answered the LORD, and said,*

2. *I know that thou canst do every thing and that there is no thought hidden from thee.*

3. *Who is he that hides counsel without knowledge?*

Now Job repeated what the Lord had said before.

He that hides counsel without knowledge is following the order of Leviathan in spite of the fact that he says it is the other way around. Even though they came as three friends of Job, they were really agents of the system of Leviathan, which had trapped and enslaved them. They did not come to Job with the counsel of God during his time of testing. Instead of consoling him, they became a major part of the test. And in the end, God used Job to set them free.

> *Religious leaders who only hear the voice of God (and they think that this is a big deal) yet do not see, continue to be blind guides of the blind.*

3. *Therefore, I have denounced that which I did not understand, things too wonderful for me, which I did not know.*

Job did not know. He did not understand the conflict and how God intended to manifest Himself to him.

4. *Hear, now, and I will speak; I will ask of thee, and thou shalt cause me to know.*

Before, Job had wanted to explain his case, his righteousness. Now, however, he only wants to listen. He wants God to cause him to know.

5. *With my ears I had heard thee; but now my eyes see thee.*

Religious leaders who only hear the voice of God (and they think that this is a big deal) yet do not see, continue to be blind guides of the blind. And the Lord says that if the blind lead the blind, both will wind up in the same pit. This is the pit of the insatiable desires of the natural man, and the entire order of Leviathan is bound to this realm. The devil is bound to this realm with all his followers. No matter how religious they pretend to be, they can never break free from the order of the belly, the navel, and the natural carnal appetites. They will never be able to stop crawling around in the dust of the Adamic nature. Even if they come up out of the sea (symbol of the nations), they will remain in the realm of the dust. They cannot fly, for they will never have the wings of the dove of the Spirit of God.

6. *Therefore, I abhor myself and repent in dust and ashes.*

7. *And it was so, that after the LORD had spoken these words unto Job, the LORD said to Eliphaz, the Temanite, My wrath has been kindled against thee, and against thy two friends; for ye have not spoken by me in uprightness, as my slave Job has.*

Look at this now from God's point of view. He did not tell them that what they said was not correct. The letter to Timothy says that all Scripture is profitable for doctrine, for reproof, and for instruction in righteousness. This includes the words of Eliphaz the Temanite and those of his two friends recorded in the book of Job. All of this has application.

It is true that people are suffering because of hidden sin in their lives and that they must repent of their sin in order to go forward. But because this is often the case, Eliphaz thought that it was always the case, so he was mistaken in regard to Job. Eliphaz did not say what he said because he was walking in uprightness; he was, rather, defending the system. Job had said some things that had to be corrected afterwards. Job had wanted to argue with God, when in reality, Job had made a previous covenant with God (where he had surrendered everything to God) and therefore had no right to contend with God even if God killed him. So Job repented in dust and ashes. But God said that it was Eliphaz and his two friends who did not speak by God in uprightness.

> 8. *Therefore, take unto you now seven bullocks and seven rams, and go to my slave Job, and offer up for yourselves a burnt offering; and my slave Job shall pray for you; for only because I will accept him, I shall not deal with you according to your folly, in that ye have not spoken by me in uprightness, like my slave Job.*

God ordered them to present themselves with seven bullocks. This is a symbol of completely surrendering their walk in the flesh to the Lord. Then they had to take seven rams. This is a symbol of all the guilt management that the religious system loves to impose. All of this must be bled to death on the altar so the power of sin and guilt is done away with. The system of Leviathan must have the life taken out of it. Seven bullocks and seven rams mean the totality of sin and guilt that God wants dead. God wants us dead to sin, and He also wants the guilt dead so that the enemy will no longer have any hold on us.

Then Job prayed for them as the holocaust of the burnt offering ascended (remember that this is the link between heaven and earth). Even so, the Lord did not say He would receive them. He said that He would receive Job. He would receive the true body of Christ represented by Job.

God will have a holy nation, a royal priesthood, who will be able to intercede for these problems and for these persons who are linked into the system of Leviathan and doing everything backwards while convinced that they are serving God. Jesus said that many of His true followers would be persecuted or killed, and the ones doing the persecution would think that they were doing a great service to God. But now we are at the time when the Lord wants to dismantle the system of Leviathan, and this is how He is going to do it:

He will only accept the Lord Jesus Christ. The only provision for us is in Him. It is Christ in you, the hope of glory (Colossians 1:27).

> 9. *So Eliphaz, the Temanite, and Bildad, the Shuhite, and Zophar, the Naamathite, went, and did according as the LORD commanded them; and the LORD accepted Job.*

> 10. *And the LORD turned the captivity of Job.*

Why was Job in captivity? For his sin? No, because God allowed him to be taken into captivity before Satan and before the system of Leviathan. This is why the Lord said to His people on another day, *Come out of Babylon.* Why were the people of the Lord in Babylon? Because the Lord permitted this so that they would learn the ways of the Lord. This is how He will overcome the power of the enemy. Then comes the moment when the Lord proclaims the acceptable year of the Lord, when He proclaims liberty and everything changes. I believe that we are now entering into this new day.

> 10. *And the LORD turned the captivity of Job, when he prayed for his friends; also the LORD gave Job twice as much as he had before.*

For this reason, if we make it out of Babylon, we cannot look down on or despise those who remain behind, because God turned the captivity of Job when he prayed for his three friends who were still entangled in the system.

> 11. *Then all his brethren came unto him and all his sisters and all those that had been of his acquaintance before and ate bread with him in his house; and they condoled him and comforted him over all the evil that the LORD had brought upon him; each one also gave him an ewe, and an earring of gold.*

They received the Word of God through Job, because man shall not live by bread alone but by every word that proceeds from the mouth of God.

Why does the Lord bring evil upon His people? To purify us that we might pass the test, so we can function in the celestial realm by being pure in heart, and so we can see things as God sees them, instead of only being able to hear in the spiritual realm. The one who can hear but not see is prone to error because the devil can be speaking in a voice that seems like God. The one who cannot see can easily fall into a pit. In fact, Scripture is clear: They will fall into the pit.

The one who can hear but not see is prone to error because the devil can be speaking in a voice that seems like God.

The children of Israel gave Aaron their gold earrings and he made for them the golden calf. In the system of Leviathan, the calf is worshipped, the flesh is worshipped, man is worshipped. In the system of God, we must catch the seven bullocks and sacrifice them. We must sacrifice our complete ability to walk in the flesh and any desire to exalt or worship any other person or thing that is not God.

They each brought Job a ewe. For this remnant of God that had been sterile and passed through the trial of Job, the Word says that the time will come when none of the ewes will be sterile and they will all give birth to twins (Song of Solomon 4:2; 6:6). When the Lord has a clean remnant, He can multiply it.

12. *So the LORD blessed the latter end of Job more than his beginning; for he had fourteen thousand sheep and six thousand camels and a thousand yoke of oxen and a thousand she asses.*

I am not sure of the significance of many of these details, but one thousand yoke of oxen and one thousand she asses means that which was carnal has now entered perfection.

13. *He also had seven sons and three daughters.*

The first sons and daughters were not lost; they were safe with God. Therefore, with the new sons and daughters, Job had double. The enemy exceeded what he and God agreed on when he killed the children of Job. God had not said that Satan could do that. When the enemy overplays his hand and goes too far, this allows God to clear things up. Scripture says that God is storing all the injustice up in vials in heaven, and these vials will be poured out when the judgments of God fall upon the world. This judgment will be freedom for His true people. It is only condemnation for those who do not desire to walk in the ways of God.

Eliphaz the Temanite was wrong when he said that Job's children must have been killed because of hidden sin in their lives. God had them safe and secure in heaven. This is also the case with many millions of martyrs over the course of history.

14. *And he called the name of the first, Jemima, and the name of the second, Kezia, and the name of the third, Kerenhappuch.*

It goes on to say that in all the land no women were found as beautiful as the daughters of Job, and their father gave them an inheritance among their brethren. This is the same theme as the Song of Solomon.

The significance of these three names is very important. Jemima means "day by day." Job had learned to live day by day with the Lord. The name of the second was Kezia, or Cassia, which is one of the principle ingredients of the anointing oil and means "true praise." Job knew about true praise because when he lost everything, Scripture says he fell down on the ground and worshipped. The name of the third, Kerenhappuch, means "a horn of many colors." Keren means "horn" and Happuch means "of many colors." The horn (the shofar, the trumpet, the ram's horn) is a symbol of the power of when God speaks and the power of His creative spoken word. Also, remember Joseph (son of Jacob) was given a coat of many colors as a symbol that he was going to rule and reign (right before he was sold into slavery for thirteen years by his brothers).

Many colors are in the rainbow, which is a symbol of the covenant with God. So the person who learns to walk day by day with the Lord enters into true worship of the Lord (which has nothing to do with the things of this world, or health, or money, or talented musicians in beautiful cathedrals). True worship has to do with being in communion with the Lord and allowing God to be God in our life. This will bring us eventually to where we are in power due to being in a true covenant with the Lord. At the end, Job had that power and authority, and the true body of Christ will have the same in the end. This is the story of Job, the story of how to overcome the order of Leviathan.

The Levitical priesthood had to be replaced by the Melchisedec priesthood. The Levitical priesthood received a curse with Eli because Eli was seeking horizontal union and was unable to discipline his sons and prevent them from continuing their carnal way of doing things (1 Samuel 2:12). Only the sons of Zadok could continue the priesthood (Ezekiel 44:10-15). Melchisedec and Zadoc are from the same word, which means "righteousness." The Lord wants to make us part of His body and will make us part of His righteousness. This is the final lesson.

The only thing that can stop Leviathan is a people identified in the book of Revelation as those who *have overcome him by the blood of the Lamb and by the word of their testimony; and they loved not their lives unto the death* (Revelation 12:11). This is how they overcame him. There is no other way.

The church of Pentecost has thought that they can overcome him by using their spiritual gifts, but this is not possible. Neither can he be overcome by apostles, prophets, evangelists, pastors, or teachers. Leviathan can only be overcome by a people who follow the Lamb whithersoever He goes. By a people who have learned to hearken unto His voice only and will not follow another. By a people who know what it is to apply the truth. This is what Job did. By an overcoming people who receive the unique covering offered by the blood of the Lamb. This covering of the blood contains the life, for the life is in the blood. And the secret of being covered by the Spirit of God is having the blood applied over us. The blood cannot be applied over us if we are not willing to die to the flesh and to all carnality and to have everything else corrected in us by the Spirit of God. This is the people that will overcome. This is the tactical battle order of God. This is the only way to overcome Leviathan.

Let us pray

Lord, we ask that we might truly understand this message and that it may enter our spirit. Lord, may we desist from our own attacks on the enemy so that we may submit, Lord, to your plan, to learn your ways, to form part of your true body, and to participate in the victory even when the victory comes from apparent defeat. Lord, may we pass from the realm of only hearing your voice into the realm of being able to see things from your point of view. Lord, may we pass into the realm of being able to see you and of being changed and transformed due to being in your presence, into a realm where Leviathan is not able to function, where he has no power, where he has no experience. Lord, may we be able to operate in the realm from which he will fall and from which he will never be able to return. We ask this in the name of our Lord Jesus. Amen.

CHAPTER 4

The New Birth

The theme of this chapter is the new birth. In order to be born, there must first be a conception. And on the other hand, the fact remains that many births are frustrated by abortion. In the United States, we are told that there are about three million abortions every year. Scripture says, *Howbeit the spiritual is not first, but the natural; and afterward, that which is spiritual* (1 Corinthians 15:46). If there is a country with three million abortions per year in the natural realm, could it also be that something very terrible is taking place in the spiritual realm? What has happened? I fear that many churches have become spiritual abortion clinics.

The person who has received the seed of the Word of God and has entered into conception goes to the pastor and says, "I don't feel good."

The pastor, without understanding what the Lord has in mind, replies, "Of course you are fine. Of course you are saved. Read here. See this verse. You are saved."

The Lord would like to change many things. When someone has not yet been born again, they are still a spiritual fetus; they find themselves warming a pew in some church, but their spiritual senses are not developed. They are unable to see in the spiritual realm. They cannot eat on their own. They need to be connected to a mother religious system by an umbilical cord or they will die. I am convinced that a large number of those who claim to be Christians have never truly been born again.

After a new birth, it is necessary to be baptized in (the Greek says "into") the Holy Spirit. Without the baptism into the Holy Spirit, it is not possible to understand the ways of God. Why is it necessary to go over these themes? Because if we think everyone is born again and baptized in the Holy Spirit and we preach with this assumption, someone may hear the message but not be able to understand anything.

There is an epidemic of gifts that are born out of the natural man or that come from a religious spirit but are not from the Holy Spirit. People can speak in tongues without having the baptism of the Holy Spirit because their tongues can come from another source. Some can prophesy, yet the prophecy is not of the Holy Spirit; it has come out of the person's own heart or from another spirit. The Word says that in the last days there will be much deception (Matthew 24:3-5).

It is not enough just to believe in the Lord; we must be planted in Him. Being baptized in (into) the name of Jesus means we are to be immersed into His nature. Many times people come out of churches immersed (or sprinkled) with water. They got wet but were not immersed into the nature of Jesus. This is the reason their lives do not change afterwards. They entered a church or a denomination and fulfilled the rites of membership, but they did not enter into the nature of God.

Most of the verses in Scripture having to do with baptism speak of baptizing in (into) the name (nature) of Jesus and do not even literally mention water. In Matthew 28:19 it says, *Go ye therefore and teach all nations, baptizing them in* [Greek "into"] *the name of the Father and of the Son and of the Holy Spirit.* The name (nature) of Jesus the Son is the same nature as that of the Father and of the Holy Spirit. There is no conflict or discrepancy. The religion of men has managed to baptize people in water, but in many cases they did not get baptized into the nature of God. To be truly born again, people must receive the divine nature (2 Peter 1:4), because this is the Word that He desires to plant in us, and He is the living Word that comes to reside in our hearts.

People leave the baptismal course. They leave the confirmation class. They come out of the baptism and walk around completely defeated by sin because it is not the nature of God that has them under dominion. A corrupt seed has been planted in them instead of an incorruptible seed.

1 John 3

6. *Whosoever abides in him does not sin: whosoever sins has not seen him or known him.*

This does not jibe with the doctrine that is being preached in many churches today. None of these churches will accept that this is true. They say that even though it is written like this in the Bible, the reality has to be different because they are not experiencing this type of victory.

9. *Whosoever is born of God does not commit sin; for his seed remains in him; and he cannot sin because he is born of God.*

This verse speaks of a being born of God that is not known or experienced in most of the modern churches. In the born-again experience that is known and experienced in most churches, people continue and are even compelled to keep on sinning. So the new birth that is announced today in most of the churches is not really a birth; it is more like a "conception" in the Spirit. It produces spiritual fetuses that begin to be formed in the womb of the mother church. Now, it is true that life begins at conception, but this is not the same as being truly born again.

To be born again is to enter another realm in the Lord. In this realm people can eat on their own, separate from the mother. It is a realm where the child can see; this is very different from the darkness and obscurity of the interior of the womb. It is a realm where the child can hear clearly and with precision instead of indistinctly. It is an emerging into a realm where taste and smell function. It is a coming out of (spiritual) darkness and into brilliant light (1 Peter 2:9). Even a newborn can reject or receive a bottle, depending on temperature or taste. Some newborn babies seem to have more discernment than older folks. At least, they will not receive rotten or adulterated food.

There is a new birth in God where the person does not habitually sin, yet we do not seem to experience this. We are born again and remain a mixed-up mess. It requires a long, hard haul to come to maturity and get rid of unclean things in our lives. So if our experience does not line up with the Word of God, should we fix up the Word so it lines up with our defeat? No. God offers more than what the church is experiencing. He is offering another realm beyond the experience of the majority of Christians. There is a place in God where it is Him in us, and not us still full of our own corruption, covered over by the Holy Spirit while God works on the mess! This is what we have now, but in the Bible are many examples to the contrary.

When the Lord called Gideon, Scripture does not say the Holy Spirit clothed himself upon or over Gideon; it says, *the Spirit of the LORD clothed himself in Gideon* (Judges 6:34). This means that it was the Spirit of the Lord inside and outside clothed as Gideon, so he was clean inside. The Spirit of the Lord looked like Gideon to the eyes of men, but inside it was the Spirit of God. As the story progresses, it is clear that it had to be this way because with only three hundred men, Gideon overcame a multitude without losing any of his men. That had to be the

Spirit of the Lord because Gideon (in his human capacity) was not capable of doing this.

The Spirit of the Lord clothed himself in Gideon and went out and did battle. We have had the experience of God giving gifts and using us over the top of our problems. Likewise, Balaam's donkey was used of God to say a few words to a prophet who had lost his way (Numbers 22). However, the Lord is now getting ready to do things differently. He wants us truly born again. He wants us to be baptized, not with a little dose *of* His Spirit (Acts 2:17), but with the fullness described in Joel 2.

> *The time is come when things will be done God's way, because the day of man taking the things of God and making them work man's way is over.*

Peter quoted Joel, but instead of saying, *I will pour out my Spirit*, he says, *I will pour out of my Spirit* because this was the Feast of Firstfruits (Pentecost) and not the fullness. Now comes the Feast of Tabernacles, which is the feast of fullness. The time is come when things will be done God's way, because the day of man taking the things of God and making them work man's way is over. In the day of God, the Lord does things His way, and this is completely different from what most have experienced up to this point.

We may now have the hope that there will be new births where the people will be born clean and will walk clean. While we are still here in flesh and blood, there will always be the possibility of sin. But whoever is born of God, whoever remains in God, does not sin.

1 John 2

1. *My little children, I write these things unto you, that ye sin not; and if anyone has sinned, we have an Advocate before the Father, Jesus, the righteous Christ;*

It will be painful, but He can remove sin and rebellion from us. Notice that it does not say *when* we sin, it says *if* anyone has sinned.

1 John 3

10. *In this the sons of God are manifest, and the sons of the devil: whosoever does not righteousness and that loves not his brother is not of God.*

With these criteria, where are we in the church? With all the infighting and warring of one with another, where are we? Are we born of God or of the devil?

14. *We know that we are passed from death unto life, in that we love the brethren. He that does not love his brother abides in death.*

A person who abides in death has not been born again!

15. *Whosoever hates his brother is a murderer and ye know that no murderer has eternal life abiding in him.*

16. *In this we have known the charity of God because he laid down his life for us; we also ought to lay down our lives for the brethren.*

How many people are willing to lay down their lives for their brethren? So it is clear that we are in bad trouble and many have not entered in.

Matthew 5:3-4, the Sermon on the Mount, where the Lord described the new birth and the baptism into the Holy Spirit, are two of the most key verses in Scripture. The person who does not understand these two verses will not understand much else in the Bible. They are in the context of the baptism of John. Into what was John's baptism? Scripture does not overtly even mention the water; it says *baptism unto repentance*. This amounted to taking the person and submerging them into repentance where the person would declare, "My Adamic nature is no good. I need the new nature that comes from God."

True repentance cannot be acquired without a miracle of the grace of God. This is repentance above and beyond our human capacity, because whoever receives this baptism will be able to understand the plan and purpose of God in Jesus Christ. Luke 3 says that John came preaching the baptism of (Greek "into") repentance for the remission of sins (Luke 3:3), and whoever would not receive this baptism could not understand what was coming in Jesus Christ (Luke 7:29, 30).

But there is another baptism in another higher dimension, because John said, *I indeed baptize you in water unto repentance, but he that comes after me is mightier than I, whose shoes I am not worthy to bear; he shall baptize you in the Holy Spirit and fire* (Matthew 3:11; Luke 3:16). And we have experienced very little of that baptism into the fire of the Spirit of God.

Matthew 5

3. Blessed are the poor in spirit, for theirs is the kingdom of the heavens.

This is a very interesting construction. *Poor in spirit* is a spiritual phrase. This verse could be paraphrased, "Blessed are those who recognize their spiritual need," or even deeper, "Blessed are those who allow themselves to be dispossessed of their pride and arrogance." The original languages tend to invert the meaning of the phrase. *Poor in spirit* is the opposite of pride, and in Greek there is a sense of permitting that something be taken from us. We must allow God to strip us of our (spiritual) pride.

And at the end of the paraphrase, it would say, "for they (and only they) have God as their King." The word *kingdom* and the word *king* are the same, and they are translated according to use and context. The person who will not allow their arrogance or spiritual pride to be stripped away cannot have God as king because there can be only one king. We cannot be king at the same time that He is king. One of the two kings has to be up and the other down. No one can serve two masters. This matter must be resolved by allowing the Lord to do His work in us. When the Lord begins to work, and we let Him do His work in us, the result is that we can enter the kingdom of God. The kingdom of God means that He is the king instead of us. Unless this is defined, we cannot retain the Spirit of God.

> *We cannot be king at the same time that He is king.*

4. *Blessed are those that mourn, for they shall be comforted.*

Jesus said that He must return to His Father so that He might send us the Comforter (John 16:7-15). He said that He would not leave us alone as (spiritual) orphans. There are several words translated "to mourn" in the New Testament. One word means to cry out of sadness, pain, or self-pity, but in Matthew it is about something different. Here it means to mourn a death. Who are we going to mourn? The king that we used to be. If we do not mourn self being taken off of the throne of our lives, we cannot be comforted, because the Spirit of God comes to take over the authority and dominion of our being.

Let us examine Acts 5:32. This is how this verse reads in the original:

> *And we are his witnesses of these things, and so is also the Holy Spirit, whom God has given to those that persuade him.*

Other Bibles say *to those who obey him.*

So if we obey God, God will give us the Holy Spirit. But there is a problem. Without the Holy Spirit, it is impossible to obey God. And again, there is exclusiveness in the Greek, which means "only to those who do such and so." If this text really said that God gives His Holy Spirit only to those who obey Him, then we would be lost. We would have to obey God in order to obtain the Holy Spirit, and without the Holy Spirit, we cannot obey God.

This word is not the verb for "to obey." This word *obey* is used in the Scriptures in other cases. Here, however, it is the verb meaning to persuade (or to demonstrate faith in God). We must persuade God of what? We must persuade God that we desire to be in covenant with Him, that we desire to be governed by Him instead of being governed by ourselves, which actually puts us under the control of the enemy. If we manage to convince Him of this, He will give us the Holy Spirit to fulfill His part of the covenant with us. Therefore, the real Holy Spirit does not come all that easy. This is why it took ten days of intense prayer in the upper room, and all genuine revivals throughout church history are similar.

In the early church, when someone was baptized in water, much of the time it coincided with being baptized into the nature of God. The Holy Spirit fell upon the person who was saying, "I want to die to my past. I want to die to my ego. I want to die to being my own king. I accept being sown in the death of Christ so that my old nature can be undone, the power of sin can be undone in me, and I might be born again in the power of resurrection."

So God would sign the covenant and give the Spirit of God. The Holy Spirit would come on the scene as in the day of Pentecost, or as what happened to those in the house of Cornelius, or as when Philip preached to the Samaritans. Then Peter and John noticed that when the apostles laid their hands on people, they received the gift of the Holy Spirit. Remember when Simon the magician wanted to buy this gift with money (Acts 8:18, 19)?

Two hundred and fifty years ago in the Great Awakening, John Wesley preached about the difference between the gospel of the kingdom of God and the gospel of Simon the magician. Today it is the gospel of Simon the magician that seems to prevail in many places by those who seek personal gain from the gospel of God.

This is the cause of many people not being born again. They are not being born again as described in the Scriptures. They are being aborted into a terrible mixture that requires a lot of purification afterward. This is not the original plan of God. God's original plan is to birth legitimate, clean sons who will have a clean walk because the Holy Spirit is holy and is not an unclean spirit.

32. *And we are his witnesses.*

The word *witness* is the same word as *martyr* in the New Testament. The disciples who were saying this became martyrs later on. We are witnesses, witnesses unto death.

32. *And we are his witnesses of these things, and so is also the Holy Spirit, whom God has given to those that persuade him.*

To those that persuade Him, or those who desire to be in covenant with God are those who truly desire to be governed by God. These are the ones who want to persuade Him that they want Him to come in and bring down the government of self and of ego that is so deeply rooted in all of us due to being born into the nature of Adam.

If we return to Matthew 5, we can see that faith is joined to repentance. Repentance and faith help bring down the old man. We place our confidence in God. We mourn and bury the old man, knowing that now we are no longer in charge;

God will be in charge. Then the consolation of the Holy Spirit comes. *For if ye live according to the flesh, ye shall die; but if through the Spirit ye mortify the deeds of the body, ye shall live* (Romans 8:13).

    5. *Blessed are the meek, for they shall inherit the earth.*

The meek are those who obey God, and we cannot be meek and obey God without having the Holy Spirit. We must first have the Comforter (verse 4) in order to have meekness (verse 5). This is the beginning of the fruit of the Spirit in our lives. This is not something we can do on our own.

Jesus is the perfect example of meekness:

> *For he has made him to be sin for us, who knew no sin, that we might be made the righteousness of God in him* (2 Corinthians 5:21).

    6. *Blessed are those who hunger and thirst for righteousness, for they shall be satisfied.*

The person who has a hunger and a thirst for righteousness does not live by bread alone but by every word that proceeds out of the mouth of God (Matthew 4:4). They live to do what God wants. If we live to do what God wants, something must die in us, just as Jesus had to die. He laid down His body and His life, and when He died, the original Scripture says He *gave the Spirit* (Matthew 27:50; Luke 23:46; John 19:30). He gave the Spirit into the hands of His Father, and after He ascended, He could pour out the Spirit in us. This was the inheritance that He had received from the Father (John 1:32; 3:34), and He was willing to give up the Spirit so that He could die here for us (John 10:18). Now He makes us potential joint heirs of all that He had before by the Holy Spirit (Romans 8:17).

The person who does not hunger and thirst for righteousness has not been born again. If the appetites have not changed, the new birth has not taken place. Such a person attempts to renew his old life, as we see in the gospel of Simon the magician who renewed the life of Adam. Many Christian counselors are entangled in this (or at least they claim to be Christian) when they are really humanistic psychologists or psychiatrists trying to fix the problems of Adam. They try to restore the nature of Adam, saying that if we are ill it is because we suffered in childhood or someone did some damage to us, and we are innocent because this is the way that we are. Of course, they always charge a lot of money to state this.

But in the gospel of Jesus the Christ, it says that the old has to die. The old king must be brought down. Wipe out the old and have a clean slate. *Old things are passed away; behold, all things are made new* (2 Corinthians 5:17). This is a different gospel from what is being preached in many places today. This is one of the reasons I do not promote conducting baptisms as if we were working in a brick factory, putting everyone into the same mold, giving them the same course, submerging them in the water, and making them members of a given church. The Lord has demonstrated that He can baptize the person directly into the nature of God without even using any water if He so desires. Where is the real baptism into the Holy Spirit and fire promised in Matthew 3:11? Look at what Paul wrote:

1 Corinthians 1

17. *For Christ sent me **not** to baptize, but to preach the gospel, not with wisdom of words, lest the cross of Christ should be made void.*

18. *For the word of the cross is foolishness to those that perish, but unto us who are saved, it is the power of God.*

19. *For it is written, I will destroy the wisdom of the wise and will bring to nothing the understanding of the prudent.*

20. *Where is the wise? where is the scribe? where is the philosopher of this world? Has not God made foolish the wisdom of this world?*

21. *For in the wisdom of God, since the world by wisdom knew not God, it pleased God by the foolishness of preaching to save those that believe.*

God sent Paul to preach, not to baptize (and yes, Paul did admit to having baptized a few people in the preceding verses). God told Paul that it pleases God *by the foolishness of preaching to save those that believe.* I am with Paul. God has called me to preach. I am going to preach my heart out and let Him be the one to baptize! (And yes, I also admit to having baptized a few people in water as the Lord has led me on specific occasions.)

> *I am with Paul. God has called me to preach.*

The real Holy Spirit of God, God Himself, can speak through a person. When this Spirit prophesies, it is for exhortation, for consolation, and for the edification of the person as God Himself indicates. When someone prophesies by the Spirit of God, it is to exhort us to do what God is already speaking to us about, or to console or comfort us regarding something that the Lord knows in advance that we need (1 Corinthians 14:3).

The word *comfort* means "to give strength or power," to gain the power of God to do what He wants. God is edifying a body of many members, and true prophecy will motivate us to flow with the other members of the body so that there is no schism in the body. John refers to this when he says that he who hates his brother does not know God and has not seen God. In a wider sense, this person is not born again. It is not possible to love God and hate your brother. For this reason, we must be willing to receive brethren who do not have the same doctrine we do if they have the same Lord. If others do not have the same Lord, they are not our brethren because they have not been born of the same Spirit.

We cannot reject those who are born of God and have the Spirit of the Lord, even if their understanding is not well refined. What will really join us is to know that we all have the same commitment to God, and He is going to purify everything in our lives. So if there is anything that needs to be purified in any of our brethren, we have the confidence that the Lord will do it. We need not worry or be obsessed (as in the Inquisition) to make sure that only our messages, only our Bible version, or only our materials are adhered to. This is not our business. At times things must be discerned when things are not going well in the life of someone, but we must not come after anyone with our own judgments.

The Lord is the one who has absolute power by His Spirit. And if He begins the work, He is also able to finish it (if we stay with Him and remain docile). If someone has a different concept of things but holds it in good faith and is open to being corrected by the Lord whenever necessary, we can rest assured that God will correct them as necessary, just as He does with us. In the meantime, we must have faith in the Lord. When we are in a rush to precipitate judgment and condemnation, many times this is a lack of faith. It is a lack of faith because we do not have the confidence that God can deal with the situation; therefore, we are dealing with it ourselves.

If the Lord indicates that we are to give a word to someone, then we must do so in order to remain faithful to the Lord. But this is different, because after we give the word we can rest in the peace of the Lord. This is different from deciding on our own that we are going to fix everything.

I have preached in many churches where I know they have an area of blindness or where they are doing wrong. But if I go in there with a mindset and attitude of superiority, thinking I know more than they do, I will show forth arrogance and spiritual pride. In this case, my message will backfire for sure.

On the other hand, if I arrive in humility to flow with what the Lord wants without preconceived ideas of my own, knowing that if it were not for the grace of God I would undoubtedly be worse than they are, the Lord can act no matter what the problem. Many times when something really got straightened out, I was completely unaware of what the problem was and who was causing it. I gave the message. It hit the target. It caused an extremely uncomfortable moment. But it was received because they realized that God was the one who did it.

So it is essential to have the Holy Spirit that God gives to those who persuade Him (Acts 5:32). Persuade Him of what? That we want to be in covenant with God according to the manner of God. That the Word of God will be more important to us than our own word or someone else's word. Not just the written Word (which is important), but also the living Word, which is even more important. The living Word is our Lord Jesus. Only in the light of His Spirit, only with the living Word planted deep within us can we receive life from the written Word. Otherwise the letter kills.

This is necessary in order to understand what we are going to preach and to be able to receive insight when we are alone with the Lord, reading the Scriptures or meditating on His things. If you do not have this Spirit that is holy, that is pure, that will conduct us to a birth in God where the person who remains in Him does not sin, you will not come to maturity in Christ.

A final thought about these verses: *whosoever abides in Him does not sin* and *whosoever is born of God does not commit sin* (1 John 3:6, 9; 5:18). There are several words translated "sin" in the New Testament. This is not the word that means to transgress the law of God or to go against what God says. This is the Greek word *harmartia* that is a military term, erroneously defined by many scholars as "to miss the mark." He who aimed his arrow at the right target did not "sin" (*harmartia*) even if he missed the target because he was always aiming at the proper target. Those who sin are those who aim at the wrong target, even if they score a perfect bull's-eye!

This word was used in war and in practice. If in the heat of battle someone intentionally shot one of his own fellow soldiers in the back because he did not like him, it was *harmartia* even if the arrow missed. This word primarily describes a person with wrong goals, aiming to fulfill the appetites of the natural man instead of the will of God.

Maybe we will not get a perfect bull's-eye with every shot, but if we abide in Him, we will at least continue to shoot at the right target and our aim will improve with practice! Paul said that he was making an all-out effort to run the race and reach the prize of the high calling of God. He was not seeking the things of this world, nor was he seeking the glory of this world.

So he who is born of God does not sin, cannot sin, because he is on the right course seeking the right goal. This does not mean that he may not stumble on the way. In the new birth that God is offering us and in the real baptism into the real Holy Spirit, the person who enters by the *narrow gate* remains. Afterward, there is no problem with motivation or with goals. The goal is to be like Christ. The motivation is to run the race with an all-out effort to reach the prize of the high calling of God (Philippians 3:14), to come forth in the first resurrection and reign with Christ (Revelation 20:6). The goal is to overcome all of the things that Jesus Christ overcame. This does not mean that there will not be mistakes or moments of difficulty or temporary setbacks.

When you stumble or fall along the way, the direction you were facing matters, whether you were heading towards the Lord or away from Him. The Lord looks at these things. The Lord gives a hand to lift up the person who stumbled when they were going after the right goal. In the original sense of the word, this is not *harmartia*.

> *When you stumble or fall along the way, the direction you were facing matters, whether you were heading towards the Lord or away from Him.*

We could speak of other words. For example, when we practice righteousness, we are similar to an archer who repeatedly practices his marksmanship. This is what the Lord wants to do with each one of us. He wants our lives to be a constant practice of righteousness. We are to practice doing what He desires. Not just to shoot at the right target, but to excel at it. He wants to fine-tune us so we are not like a false bow that shoots arrows all over the place. We are to be a trustworthy bow in His hands. This is the will of God for each one of us (Psalm 78:9, 57).

Back in Matthew 5, after hungering and thirsting for righteousness, after receiving this change in nature (change in appetite), after being baptized into the nature of God which is at war with the nature of Adam which we were initially born with, and after having the fixed goal of following God instead of following the things of this world, what does God want from us?

Matthew 5

7. Blessed are the merciful, for they shall obtain mercy.

As we receive grace and mercy from God, He wants us to reach out to our neighbor with the same. After the new birth, our appetites change according to the will of God, and He desires that we be merciful. We must show mercy to those who have faults and problems that we may be unaware of, yet we must not deviate from our goal or from the righteousness of the nature of God.

We cannot say to a person, "Okay, continue in your homosexuality, or in your adultery, or in your dishonesty." But we can desire that God will have mercy on them – to pardon, restore, change, and convert them. If our brother asks for forgiveness, we are asked to forgive unto seventy times seven times, assuming that our brother really does desire to go forward and be changed by the Lord. (Of course there is a limit.) But we must have patience with our brother while he is persuading God that he wants to be in covenant and in a right relationship with the Lord so he might receive the Holy Spirit and be empowered to do so.

8. Blessed are the pure in heart, for they shall see God.

It is all a question of the heart. When I invite people to share on the radio, many ask me what to prepare, what is the theme. And I always give them the same answer: Prepare your heart. Come with a clean heart and see that God will bless. Blessed are those who live purifying their hearts, for they and only they shall see God.

9. Blessed are the peacemakers, for they shall be called the sons of God.

The sons of God are those of the new birth who have come to maturity. They are the peacemakers. Not like those so-called peacemakers now who say, "Well, here are two points of view and let's reconcile this down the middle."

The peacemaker of God is not like this; he does not desire to meet us in the middle. If the person is homosexual and an adulterer, you will not pacify the situation by telling him to quit the adultery and keep the homosexuality. This is not reconciliation. Reconciliation is to be righteous as God is righteous, to be just as God is just. The peacemakers in Roman times were generals in command of Roman legions. When there was trouble, they came with the army and with brute force put down the rebellion, imposing the Roman peace. These were the peacemakers. They would return to their country and make a triumphal march because they had deployed legions of troops and had completely obliterated the rebellion in a given place with overwhelming force. Scripture applies this same term to the sons of God. They are the peacemakers; they have all of the resources of the Spirit of God and can be trusted with power without limit to impose the peace of God. They are pure in heart and it is proven beyond the shadow of a doubt that Jesus Christ is their head.

This is what the Lord desires with us. He desires sons who are pure in heart, so He can apply the full force of the Spirit of God to impose the peace of God (instead of only dabbing a little anointing on those who are still immature and unclean to try to help them clean up their act). The peace of God will be imposed by force through sons of God who have experienced the new birth, are filled with the Spirit of God, and have come to maturity in Christ. Under the Lord Jesus, they have unlimited power to impose peace. The presence of the Spirit of God imposes peace. Peace is where the presence of God is, and where the presence of God is there is righteousness, and where righteousness remains there is peace.

Let us pray

Lord, we ask that we might understand the message of what is the new birth. If there is something in our lives that is not clean and is pulling us in the wrong direction, we ask, Lord, that we may be able to insist until we can persuade you that we want to be under your government, under your authority. We want to receive the fullness of the Holy Spirit who will cleanse us and produce a change in our appetites that will flow in mercy through us until we are pure in heart. Change us until we are the sons of God who will be the peacemakers that will be joint heirs with Christ. We ask this in the name of our Lord Jesus. Amen.

CHAPTER 5

Two Covenants,
Two Women,
and Two Mountains

The theme of this chapter is two covenants, two women, and two mountains. Look at Revelation 9 where the sixth angel blows the sixth trumpet. In the Scriptures in many cases, the sound of the trumpet symbolizes the voice of God. There were two types of trumpets – the metallic trumpet (silver) symbolizing the gospel of redemption, and the shofar (ram's horn trumpet) symbolizing the direct voice of the Lord. In the book of Revelation, the seven blasts of the trumpet are the direct message of God and are a call to battle for all the people of God.

Regarding our present eschatological point in time, the sixth trumpet gives a message that is parallel to the time we live in. The number six in Scripture is the number of man (Genesis 1:27, 31), and the sixth trumpet would suggest that until now we have had the message of God coming forth according to the ways of man (1 Corinthians 14:8). Without a doubt, we are now entering the seventh millennium since Adam, and the seventh millennium is the day of the Lord when the seventh trumpet will be blown.

Look what happened during the first six trumpet blasts after the message of God was given through men who on occasion have sounded an uncertain sound:

Revelation 9

20. And the rest of the men who were not killed by these plagues did not repent of the works of their hands, that they should not worship demons and the images of gold and of silver and of brass and of stone and of wood, which neither can see nor hear nor walk.

21. And they did not repent of their murders nor of their witchcraft nor of their fornication nor of their thefts.

Today we have a small remnant that is faithful to the Lord, while most of humanity is in the situation described by the above text. Humanity has not repented. The message of the Lord has not penetrated; it has bounced off most of them. We are in a time similar to when the children of Israel left Gilgal. Gilgal was the site of the second circumcision (representing the circumcision of the heart). This is a symbol of when we begin to enter into our inheritance in God, which begins by crossing the Jordan River (symbol of death to everything in us that is not of God).

The children of Israel left Gilgal and headed towards Jericho. Daily they marched once around Jericho blowing a shofar for six days. But on the seventh day, they did not just blow the seventh trumpet.

Joshua 6

4. And seven priests shall bear before the ark seven shofarot [rams' horn trumpets] of jubilee; and the seventh day ye shall go around the city seven times, and the priests shall blow with the shofarot.

5. *And when they make a long sound of jubilee with the horn so that ye hear the voice of the shofar, all the people shall shout with a great shout; and the wall of the city shall fall down flat; then the people shall ascend up each man straight before him.*

The city of Jericho symbolizes the city of religion. It is a city where men do the things of God their own way. And the Lord decided to destroy the citizens of Jericho and give the Promised Land to a people who had learned to walk according to the ways of the Lord, a people who had not only been circumcised in their flesh but also in their heart. These people had an open ear to hear and obey God (Joshua 6).

The Lord had *cut* a covenant with Abraham (back when He was called Abram), and Abram had to cut some animals down the middle (except the birds which were also offered but were not cut in half) and place them in the way. *And when the fowls came down upon the carcases, Abram drove them away* (Genesis 15:11). Every time we try to enter into covenant with God, the demons come and attempt to wreak havoc. They try to take something or to add something. The covenant of Abraham, represented by these animals, reveals the flesh, the carnal nature of the old man, which must die.

This was the reason behind the blood sacrifices. This was why the animals had to be cut down the middle. But God does not want to kill the soul of man, and this is why the birds (which symbolize the soul) were left intact. The turtledove and the young pigeon were left intact, symbolizing the place in the soul where the Holy Spirit will dwell. The Lord did not come to kill our soul; He came to restore our soul (Psalm 23:3).

What must be restored in our soul? All of our personality, our will, our emotions, our manner of thinking, our feelings, and so on. All of this is in our soul and must be restored by the power of God after the control of the flesh is cut.

In Hebrew, it does not say that God made a covenant with Abraham; it says that God *cut* a covenant with Abraham. To enter into this type of covenant with God, the sword of the truth, which is the Word of God, must enter and cut. This is something that we are unable to do on our own. In the case of Abraham, once these animals were in position, as the sun went down, *a deep sleep* came over him and *a horror of great darkness* descended upon him. And while Abraham slept, God came upon the scene and began to walk between the pieces of the sacrifice. This was to show us that we are incapable of making the necessary sacrifice. God Himself had to come in human flesh like ours and make the sacrifice. The Lord was to be the real sacrifice.

It is very important to understand what happened with Abraham. We are told that the circumcision came as a sign and a seal of the righteousness by faith that Abraham had before he was circumcised (Romans 4). God made a covenant with Abraham, and after the covenant came the circumcision. We are not capable of obeying the Lord on our own when we come before Him.

As previously explained, Acts 5:32 says that the Lord gives His Holy Spirit to those who *persuade* Him, not to those who obey Him, because we are incapable of obedience in our natural state. But we can convince God that we desire to be in covenant with Him. And if He is persuaded, He will come and cut a covenant in our heart and place His Spirit in us. This is the only way that we will ever be able to please Him.

In the desert, the people of God were shown two options:

Deuteronomy 11

29. And it shall come to pass when the LORD thy God has brought thee in unto the land where thou goest to inherit it that thou shalt put the blessing upon Mount Gerizim and the curse upon Mount Ebal.

We are entering the seventh millennium and this is when God is going to give an inheritance to His true people. We are leaving Gilgal, heading for Jericho, and the moment is impending when we will have to choose between the blessing (Mount Gerizim) or the curse (Mount Ebal). It is sad that God's people have always chosen the curse. In the example of when the covenant of law was given, it is written that the children of Israel told the Lord that they could not stand to hear His voice any longer. They told Moses to go up the mountain of God, listen to Him, and come back and tell them what God wanted them to do (Deuteronomy 5:25). Only hearing a secondhand word from the Lord will always turn into a curse because we will never be able to comply if we do not personally hear His voice. Without direct access to the voice of God, we remain lost.

We are entering the seventh millennium and this is when God is going to give an inheritance to His true people.

Abraham, known as the friend of God, walked with the Lord. He listened to the Lord when the Lord asked for his son. God's request was something seemingly impossible and unthinkable. The Lord told Abraham to sacrifice his son Isaac. Yet even then, Abraham had his faith and confidence in God. The Scriptures say that Abraham *believed the LORD, and he counted it to him for righteousness* (Genesis 15:6). Abraham was justified because he heard, and because he heard directly from the Lord, he was able to obey. But those who heard secondhand, from Moses, did not obey, and they all died in the desert while God prepared another generation that would enter into the Promised Land.

Gerizim means "to be cut." It is the mountain where the covenant with God is made, where He comes in and cuts what must be cut in our heart so we will no longer be controlled by our own whims. Ebal means "without hair, or bald." Hair is a symbol of glory, and depending on use, it can also represent arrogance. When God wanted the prophet Ezekiel to pay attention, He picked him up by the locks of his hair, by his Jewish pride, and suspended him between heaven and earth to show him the abominations that were taking place in the temple (Ezekiel 8:3).

For the covenant of law which man cannot fulfill on his own will always turn into abomination and damnation. For this reason, God provided a New Covenant. This is why the Lord Jesus came to establish a New Testament, and this is why He sealed it with His own death as the sacrifice. Without the death of the one making the will or testament, the covenant will not go into effect (Hebrews 9:16, 17). Therefore, the Lord died so we can have the inheritance of the Spirit of God living inside us.

After three years of ministry, the Pharisees and the leaders of the Jewish system had profoundly rejected the ministry of the Lord Jesus. And as Jesus left the temple for the last time (they had rejected Him and His message), He saw a fig tree beside the road and desired to eat some figs but could find none (and you know the rest of that story). There were plenty of leaves but no fruit. It has been said that when Adam and Eve covered themselves with fig leaves immediately after the fall, this was man's first attempt at religion. Then God instituted the real religion that has to do with a blood sacrifice where the nature of man must die so the life of God can enter (Genesis 3).

Restoring the altar and the application of the blood at the altar is where we receive the Spirit because the life is in the blood (Genesis 9:4; Leviticus 17:11, 14; Deuteronomy 12:23). The altar represents God's conditions for us to draw near to Him; He demands a total surrender. It is obligatory to surrender our sin and our guilt, and then we may voluntarily decide if we will surrender our very person over to Him in a burnt offering or holocaust.

This word means to ascend, and as in the case of its first use regarding Jacob's ladder, it is the connection between heaven and earth. This is the word used when the angel ascended toward heaven (in the flame of the holocaust) before the parents of Samson. This is the same thing that happened when the Lord Jesus ratified himself as the Lamb of God in the Jordan River.

The Lord Jesus submitted to the baptism (which is a symbol of death) and walked the rest of His life in the way (and shadow) of the cross. At the time of His baptism, the heavens were opened; a true holocaust will always open the heavens. And because of not having the altar or the holocaust restored, the heavens are not open for large sectors of the church. Much of the church has turned the New Covenant into an Old Covenant. The veil was torn from top to bottom, but it has been sewn from the bottom back up to the top to reintroduce an intermediary clerical class between the people and God that demands tithes and does other things that should have passed away with the passing of the covenant of law.

However, the Lord is again allowing the gospel of complete surrender to Him to be preached. And the person who is led by the Spirit of the Lord will give much more than a tithe. This person will be willing to give everything, even their own life for their brethren. The Law cannot produce people willing to give their life. In the letter to the Hebrews, the apostle makes it clear that the Law can never justify the flesh. The Law is only a shadow of that which was to come. The Levitical priesthood must be exchanged for the priesthood of Melchisedec, which is the priesthood of Christ, the priesthood of all believers.

Instead of the law of sin and death, we have the law of liberty and of life. The apostle James says we will be judged by the perfect law of liberty (James 2:12). The law of what kind of liberty? This is not the law of licentiousness. It is the law of liberty to do the will of the Lord, for where the Spirit of the Lord is, there is liberty. It is liberty to do the will of God and not to do our own will. For if we are in covenant with the Lord, our will has been circumcised, so now we desire His will.

Sadly, much of the church has chosen Mount Ebal. They have chosen the mount with no glory because it is a mount that they can control.

Sadly, much of the church has chosen Mount Ebal. They have chosen the mount with no glory because it is a mount that they can control. The Lord found no fruit on the fig tree; neither has He been able to find fruit in this church. The Lord cursed the fig tree and said, *Let no fruit grow on thee from now on for ever. Never again shall anyone eat fruit of thee hereafter for ever* (Matthew 21:19; Mark 11:14). And the next day, the fig tree had dried up from the roots.

It is very important to understand where the root of the phrase *fig tree* comes from, because the fig tree is a symbol of the people of God who desire a second-hand revelation. The curse of the Lord dried up the fig tree from its very roots, and the Lord said that there would never be any fruit. Religious rites and ceremonies of the Law cannot produce fruit. Only a covenant cut in the heart can bring forth fruit. Mount Gerizim represents this covenant.

After He cursed the fig tree, after the fig tree dried up from the roots, the Lord said something very interesting:

Mark 11

23. *For verily I say unto you that whosoever shall say to this mountain, Remove thyself and cast thyself into the sea, and shall not doubt in his heart but shall believe that what he says shall be done whatsoever he says shall be done unto him.*

Why would the Lord include these words right after cursing the fig tree? What does *this mountain* have to do with the fig tree? Paul wrote to the Galatians about the difference between law and grace. The law is the covenant of Mount Sinai of which Mount Ebal is a symbol. It is a law that man can try to fulfill out of his human nature without having a covenant cut by God in his heart.

Galatians 4

21. *Tell me, ye that desire to be under the law, have ye not heard the law?*

22. *For it is written that Abraham had two sons, the one by a bondmaid, the other by a freewoman.*

23. *But he who was of the bondwoman was born according to the flesh, but he of the freewoman was born through the promise.*

24. *Which things are an allegory; for these women are the two covenants: the one from the Mount Sinai, which begat unto slavery, which is Hagar.*

Sarah and Hagar are the two covenants – one by the flesh and the other by the promise. In this passage, Paul makes it very clear that the natural Jew who is trying to fulfill the covenant of law that was given on Mount Sinai is really tied to the Egyptian slave woman.

> 25. *For this Hagar or Sinai is a mount in Arabia, which corresponds to the one that is now Jerusalem.*

No wonder the Jews wanted to kill Paul! He said that in the eyes of the Lord, those of Jerusalem were really Arabs. This provoked the same kind of fury that was produced in the hearts of those on the council who listened to Stephen when they descended on him and killed him after he gave them a word from the Lord. Scripture says, *When they heard these things, they were divided [cut] in their hearts* (Acts 7:54). When Peter stood up on the day of Pentecost and spoke, Scripture uses the same word to describe the reaction, but they said, *what shall we do? Then Peter said unto them, Repent and be baptized each one of you into the name of Jesus Christ for the remission of sins, and ye shall receive the gift of the Holy Spirit.* And three thousand believed (Acts 2:37, 38). When the Word comes forth with power, it produces these results.

> 25. *which together with her children is in slavery.*

When the Lord insinuated to the Jews that they were in slavery and He could set them free, they got angry and said, *We are Abraham's seed, and we have never served anyone* (John 8:33).

They had forgotten about all that happened to them in Babylon. They were not even aware that with all their effort to fulfill the Law and the sacrifices, they continued in slavery to sin. Most of the church continues in slavery to sin because they continue under the covenant of the curse instead of choosing the covenant of blessing.

> 26. *But the Jerusalem of above is free, which is the mother of us all.*

When we are born again in the Spirit, we are born into the nature of God. Now we no longer belong to the earthly Jerusalem but to the heavenly Jerusalem. Natural, earthly Jerusalem has two options – to continue to be part of that represented by Mount Sinai by having chosen Mount Ebal (it is also identified with Sodom and Egypt), or to become Sion (the dwelling place of God).

There is another contrast with two mountains – one is Mount Hermon and the other is Mount Sinai. Sinai is the covenant of law while Hermon is the covenant of the grace of the Lord. Deuteronomy 4:48 says, *even unto Mount Sion, which is Hermon.*

In Psalm 65:1 it says, *Praise doth rest in thee, O God, in Sion, and unto thee shall the vow be performed.* This is another reference, spelled Sion, which is Hermon. What if praise were to be confined to natural Jerusalem and we all had to go there in order to properly worship the Lord? No, our Jerusalem is the heavenly Jerusalem; therefore, we can worship in spirit and in truth and not in any particular place. The Lord Jesus told the Samaritan woman:

> *Woman, believe me, the hour comes when neither in this mountain nor in Jerusalem shall ye worship the Father* (John 4:21).

In the Old Testament, there are 153 verses that make reference to Zion. This is referring directly to natural Jerusalem, which may or may not be the actual dwelling place of God depending on which covenant we are referring to. There are nine OT quotes in the NT referring to Zion and all of them are spelled with the Greek letter Sigma instead of Zeta (they are literally spelled Sion instead of Zion).

> *as the dew of Hermon, that descends upon the mountains of Zion; for there the LORD commands blessing and eternal life* (Psalm 133:3).

This helps to clear up the meaning of Hermon, which is the highest mountain in the Promised Land but is not in the hands of the natural Jews today. The spiritual equivalent is not in the hands of the church either. Many times natural Israel gives a good picture in the natural realm of what is going on with the church in the spiritual realm.

The Holy Land is also a map of what our life can be in God. We begin in the Dead Sea of sin with our journey up the Jordan River (which represents the dealings of God in our lives to kill off everything that is not of Him to bring about the death of the old man, of the old nature). We arrive at the Sea of Galilee, which represents life in the Spirit. There is life here, and fish. This is where Jesus' ministry was centered. If we continue upstream according to Proverbs 15:24:

> The way of life is uphill to the wise, that he may separate himself from Sheol below.

We want to get as far away from sin and death as possible, so we continue up the rapids and waterfalls of the Jordan. The Jordan is born high upon snow-covered Mount Hermon, which represents the holiness of being separated for the exclusive use of the Lord. This is where the bride comes with her husband in the Song of Solomon (Song of Solomon 4:8).

So which mountain, if we have faith, shall be thrown in the sea? Ebal and Sinai or Hermon and Gerizim?

The truth is that the Lord wants us to have an encounter with Him in the mountain of His holiness. He wants us by faith to tell the other mountain to throw itself into the sea. The system of rites, of guilt trips, and of controlling the people with an intermediary priesthood is not the priesthood of Melchisedec. Melchisedec means "king of righteousness" and is from the root word *Zadok*, and the sons of Zadok are the only priests who will be allowed to minister in the presence of God when

He establishes His government on earth. The other priests are under a curse and are cut off. This was the sentence on the house of Eli. When Solomon built the temple, the line of Eli was overthrown, and Zadok was put in place as a symbol of what would come in the future of the restoration in the kingdom of God here on earth (See 1 Kings 1-4).

In past messages on Revelation, I had shared regarding the seals, in that first it is necessary that the covenant of God – the message that will sound through the trumpets – be unsealed and that this is the work of the Spirit of God. And when the Lord Jesus opens the seals as a result, the heavens open for those who are in covenant with God. This is the holocaust

This is the holocaust of our lives, to be living sacrifices.

of our lives, to be living sacrifices. Romans 12 indicates that our soul, our being, will be restored so that we can participate in sounding the trumpets.

In Revelation 10, an angel descends from heaven with a rainbow over his head. The rainbow symbolizes a covenant with God. This light of God is divided into seven colors. This is the sign of the covenant of God with every living thing (see Genesis 9:12, 13), and this covenant has become fulfilled now with an angel who has his head in the heavens and his feet here on earth. This describes the body of Christ. The angel is clothed with a cloud (water vapor which represents the very nature of God, see Genesis 2:6).

The first Feast of the Passover, linked to the Law, is symbolized many times in Scripture as ice. It is there, but it cannot move and it cannot flow. The promises of God are frozen and we cannot seem to appropriate them. Nevertheless, with the baptism in the Holy Spirit and the fire of God, things begin to heat up and the ice begins to melt and the water begins to flow.

Through the baptism of the Holy Spirit and the circumcision of Christ in our hearts, rivers of living water can flow out of our innermost being just as they flowed out of His side.

God did not form Eve out of Adam's rib. The original text from Genesis 2 says:

> 21. *And the LORD God caused a deep sleep to fall upon Adam, and he slept; and he took one of his sides and closed up the flesh in its place;*

> 22. *and the LORD God built that which he had taken from the side of the man into a woman and brought her unto the man.*

The same thing happened when they opened one of the sides of the Lord with a lance and water and blood flowed out. With this water and blood there is a covenant of blessing (for all those born of water and of blood), and with this covenant of blessing the bride of the new Adam (Christ) is formed (I John 5:6-9). We, as the true church, are not formed out of one of Jesus' ribs; we are formed out of the water and blood that flowed from His side. We are formed by having His blood (life) applied over us and by the washing of water by the Word (His Word).

The angel has an open scroll in his hand, with one foot on the land (the people of God) and one foot on the sea (the nations). And when he opens his mouth, seven thunders sound. John was not allowed to write down those seven thunders because those seven thunders were seven trumpet blasts of the voice of God all at once. This was the mystery of God, the secret of God reserved until the end of the times. But when the seventh trumpet begins to sound, the mystery of God will be finished (Revelation 10:7).

We are entering into the seventh millennium and this is the moment when the Lord is revealing this truth. The seventh angel is not like the vision of Nebuchadnezzar, which was an image with a head of gold but with feet of clay mixed with iron (of the law mixed with human nature), which could not walk or function. The feet of the seventh angel, which are a faithful remnant of the Lord here on earth, remain as brilliant pillars of fire. They blaze with the fire of God, and there is no degradation in this body. They operate in the same nature as the Lord Jesus, the same nature as the head functioning with the feet.

Then it speaks of two witnesses who give testimony. *And if anyone desires to hurt them, fire proceeds out of their mouth and devours their enemies; and if anyone desires to hurt them, he must in this manner be killed* (Revelation 11:5). Not so with the church that has returned to the first covenant; she has to flee.

There are people of God who do not have to flee from the enemy. There are people of God of the same quality as Jesus Christ, because they do not live to do their own will but to do His will as He came to do His Father's will. This is why the heavens are open unto them. God wanted to open the heavens for those who will participate in the ministry of the seventh angel.

Revelation 8

7. The first angel sounded the trumpet, and there followed hail and fire mingled with blood, and they were cast upon the land; and the third part of the trees was burnt up, and all green grass was burnt up.

There is an entire message in this verse. The green grass is mentioned in sixty-six verses, and there are sixty-six books in the Bible. Sixty-six is the number that identifies the written Word of the Lord. The church has had the written Word, and many use it to feed their own nature. Just as an ox fattens itself eating grass, so the people feed on the Word of God to get what they want. But when this trumpet sounds, all the green grass will burn up. Anyone who was using the things of God to sustain their existence in the flesh will be without food. It will be as in the days of Joseph in Egypt when all the grass dried up and everyone had to sell their animals to Joseph (Genesis 47:15-17). To remain alive, people will have to surrender their walk in the flesh to the Lord or they will starve to death spiritually.

When the first trumpet is blown, a third of the trees are burned up. Three is the number that has to do with the dry land. On the third day of creation, God separated the land from the sea (later God also separated His people from the nations). There are many who have been separated from the nations but still have problems. They grow as the cedars of Lebanon and become proud and arrogant. These are soon burned up on the day of the Lord.

Speaking of grass, Scripture speaks of three stages to the harvest:

Mark 4

28. *For the earth brings forth fruit of herself: first the blade* [or grass], *then the ear, after that the full grain on the ear.*

Isaiah 40

8. *The grass withers, the open flower fades; but the word of our God shall stand for ever.*

This is speaking of a word that is not only written but has become a part of our being. It has come to maturity and produced the fruit of righteousness. The apostle Peter quoted this verse from Isaiah 40.

1 Peter 1

24. *For all flesh is as grass, and all the glory of man as the flower of grass. The grass withers, and its flower falls away,*

> 25. *but the word of the Lord endures for ever. And this*
> *is the word which by the gospel is preached unto you.*

Peter was not talking about a gospel of grass or a gospel of an open flower (referring to gifts). It was the gospel of the fruit of righteousness and the seed is in the fruit. Jesus is the grain of wheat that fell into the ground and died in order to produce a great harvest in kind (John 12:24).

Jesus is the grain of wheat that fell into the ground and died in order to produce a great harvest in kind (John 12:24).

Those who evangelize under the Old Covenant can cause a lot of trouble planting corruptible (immature) seed.

Matthew 23

> 15. *Woe unto you, scribes and Pharisees, hypocrites!*
> *for ye compass sea and land to make one proselyte,*
> *and when he is made, ye make him twofold more a*
> *son of hell than yourselves.*

But those who have come to maturity in Christ can plant incorruptible seed. The Lord set the example. He planted His own life.

The person who is not willing to do the same is not worthy to preach the gospel of the kingdom of God. Scripture indicates that the woman who broke the alabaster box and poured the costly ointment on Jesus' head will be mentioned wherever this gospel is preached. Not any gospel, but this gospel of the kingdom is the gospel that is preached with great sacrifice by those willing to give everything. This is how the house of Simon the leper was filled with the wonderful odor of redemption.

Matthew 26

13. Verily I say unto you, Wherever this gospel shall be preached in the whole world, there shall also this, that this woman has done, be told for a memorial of her.

Revelation 8

8. And the second angel sounded the trumpet, and as it were a great mountain burning with fire was cast into the sea, and the third part of the sea became blood.

This is the prophetic fulfillment of what the Lord Jesus announced in the gospel:

Mark 11

23. For verily I say unto you that whosoever shall say unto this mountain, Remove thyself and cast thyself into the sea, and shall not doubt in his heart but shall believe that what he says shall be done whatsoever he says shall be done unto him.

The Lord is seeking a people who can speak to the system of this world that has tied up the church and has tied up Israel (the people of God) from the beginning. He is seeking a people who can say to Mount Sinai, to Mount Ebal, *Remove thyself and cast thyself into the sea!* For the people of God, the remnant of the Lord, have chosen the way of Mount Gerizim, of Mount Hermon, of the cross, of the holocaust, of an open heaven, and of the blessing of God.

Revelation 8

9. and the third part of the creatures which were in the sea, and had life, died; and the third part of the ships were destroyed.

When this system is thrown into the sea, it affects the sea. When these trumpets are sounded God's way by a clean people as represented by the seventh angel (this angel has the same references and description as the glorious Jesus Christ in Revelation 1), the desired effect will take place. So the results in the sea can be seen from two different perspectives. Many think that the book of Revelation is a book of damnation and destruction; nevertheless, it is also a book of blessing because it is the revelation of our Lord Jesus Christ. In the same manner, the effect that is produced when the vast mountain throws itself into the sea can be interpreted as a tremendous judgment or as tremendous salvation.

Up until now, the message of the trumpets was only affecting the land (the people of God), but now it affects the sea (the world and the nations). Remember that with the plagues of Egypt, there was a crop that was destroyed by the hail and another that was not. The barley was destroyed, and barley is a symbol of Pentecost (of the church age). But the wheat was left intact, and wheat is a symbol of tabernacles (the coming age of fullness). There are people who use barley as food, but others use it to brew beer and get drunk. Colombia has a lot of trouble with barley.

I see no problem with having a beer over lunch. But thirty beers in a cantina, when the wife and kids are suffering is a problem, without mentioning the brawls that many times result. In the same manner, the church has a problem with the gifts of the Spirit. They have used them to get drunk and to seek the personal and corporate gain of their own kingdoms. Others, horrified at the spectacle and disaster (as discernment has broken down and legions of unclean spirits wreak havoc in a church that sold its birthright and is hard to distinguish from a zoo or a circus) become spiritual teetotalers, denying that the baptism of the Holy Spirit is for today and claiming that miracles and gifts died out with the original apostles. All of this happens because none of them had the faith to tell this mountain to *Remove thyself and cast thyself into the sea.*

Now is the time for this mountain to be told to cast itself into the sea. This can only be accomplished by those who have faith. What is faith?

Romans 10

17. So then faith comes by hearing, and the ear to hear by the word of God.

The one who hears directly from God can fulfill the Word of God if the word is embraced with faith. The one who hears secondhand will remain under the curse. To hear directly from God has a price. It is the same price the Lord paid. There were two sacrifices each day – one in the morning and one in the evening. With His death, the Lord Jesus fulfilled the morning sacrifice, and if we are truly following Him, we could become part of the evening sacrifice.

The two witnesses have a spectacular ministry, but their ministry ends the same as Jesus' earthly ministry – they die. Where? In Jerusalem, the city that is linked to Sodom and Egypt, where also our Lord was crucified (Revelation 11:8). Egypt is a symbol of law and slavery and the iron dominion of Pharaoh. Sodom is linked with homosexuality, but the Bible does not say that this was the root of the problem (it was a defining symptom).

Ezekiel 16

49. Behold, this was the iniquity of thy sister Sodom: pride, fullness of bread, and abundance of idleness was in her and in her daughters, neither did she strengthen the hand of the afflicted and needy.

50. *And they filled themselves with arrogance and committed abomination before me, and when I saw it I took them away.*

The problem of Israel is the same problem as the church, and sexual deviation is a result of their sin. They look for pleasure without responsibility and without any possibility of having children. We see a church today that for the most part is not producing upstanding children of God. They are playing with gifts and ministries. They are seeking much diversion and prosperity, but in most places they are not producing clean sons of God. To produce clean sons of God there must be a clean mother and an incorruptible seed that only comes from the Lord Jesus. But this seed has not been planted in many situations. It cannot be obtained from doctrine or even from gifts. It must be obtained directly from God.

> *The problem of Israel is the same problem as the church, and sexual deviation is a result of their sin.*

Abraham and Sarah made a terrible mistake trying to help God fulfill His promise to provide them with a son who was to be their heir and heir to the promise of God. They decided to use Hagar, the Egyptian slave, since Sarah thought she was too old.

Sarah laughed when she overheard God say that she would have a son at ninety years of age. Nine months later, God had the last laugh, and the son was named Isaac (meaning "laughter").

Abraham came to the place of being willing to follow God no matter what and do exactly what God said. He was even willing to sacrifice his beloved Isaac at the word of the Lord, but God spared Isaac at the last minute. God would give His own Son. There is an interesting play on words:

Genesis 22

7. *Then Isaac spoke unto Abraham his father and said, My father; and he said, Here am I, my son. And he said, Behold the fire and the wood, but where is the lamb for the burnt offering* [holocaust]?

8. *And Abraham answered, My son,* **God will provide himself** *a lamb for a burnt offering, so they both went on together* (emphasis added).

God will provide himself meant that He Himself would be the sacrifice. God the Father would send God the Son. This sacrifice is to show us the way. The sacrifice continues to be us as we follow in His footsteps. This is the way to an open heaven and a walk in the power and authority of Christ here on the earth.

If we do not have an open heaven, if we have not understood about the burnt offering (holocaust), and if we have not understood about being living sacrifices, then we can speak to the mountain all we want and nothing will happen. For this reason, the heavens are still as brass before many. But if we do understand about the holocaust, if we do understand about being dead to sin, and if Christ truly lives in us and His faith comes forth in and through us, then we can tell the mountain to throw itself into the sea and it will comply. This desire will be manifest wherever there is communion between brethren. It will be the desire to never return to the first covenant, to never, ever implement the covenant of the law of sin and death. To choose Gerizim and not Ebal, Hermon, and not Sinai, means that Sarah, the free woman representing the Jerusalem from above, is to be the mother of us all (Galatians 4:26).

Psalm 133 – A Song of Degrees of David

1. *Behold, how good and how pleasant it is for brethren to dwell together in unity!*

This does not mean with an intermediary priesthood on top looking down on everyone else, but with the priesthood of all believers under the headship of the Lord Jesus Christ, of the order of Melchisedec as high priest forever.

> 2. *It is like the precious ointment upon the head, that runs down upon the beard, even Aaron's beard, that goes down to the skirts of his garments;*

This is not a little touch or dab of anointing, but an unlimited anointing. In the words of John the Baptist, *For he whom God has sent speaks the words of God; for God does not give the Spirit by measure unto him* (John 3:34). Many attempt to serve the Lord who were never sent by Him; therefore, they do not have the anointing to face the problems that arise.

> 3. *as the dew of Hermon,*

Hermon is the highest snow-covered mountain in the Promised Land, at the head of the Jordan River.

> 3. *...that descends upon the mountains of Zion; for there the LORD commands blessing and eternal life.*

It is sad to see all the terrible infighting among those calling themselves the people of God. If there is really only *one Lord, one faith, one baptism* (Ephesians 4:5), there should not be this conflict. I am not preaching the ecumenism that says that everyone is right in some degree and that Jesus is not the only way. The word ecumenical means "in the family." There are only two families that matter – the family of fallen Adam and the family of the risen Christ. God wants us to be part of His family and Jesus is the only way. God is the only one who is right, so we must receive the Lord Jesus Christ and submit to the discipline of God if we are to mature as His sons.

The feasts of the Lord were celebrated in Jerusalem and were also called feasts of ascent or of degrees because participants had to walk uphill to Jerusalem. And as they ascended, they sang special Songs of Degrees (there are fifteen among the Psalms).

Psalm 127 – A Song of Degrees for Solomon (Peace Offering or Holocaust)

1. *Unless the LORD builds the house, they labour in vain that build it; unless the LORD keeps the city, the watchmen watch in vain.*

This is what they would be singing as they went up to Jerusalem to celebrate the Passover or Pentecost or the Feast of Tabernacles. And even so, they did not understand that it was necessary to walk with the Lord in order for these things to be realized.

We desire to be born (again) of the Jerusalem from above. We desire to be the sons of the free woman of the promise. We desire the New Covenant.

Let us pray

Heavenly Father, we ask that we might have the faith and the dependence on you to follow you unto the ultimate consequences. We desire to say to that mountain, "Cast thyself into the sea." For your new day, we no longer desire religiosity; we do not want more rites and regulations. We want the law of liberty, the law of love written on our heart. We do not want to return to a covenant centered on human control and meetings, but a covenant centered on a daily walk with you. We want to walk towards the mountain of your holiness. We ask this in the name of our Lord Jesus. Amen.

CHAPTER 6

The Seventh Trumpet and the Seven Thunders

———————————⊶⊷———————————

In the book of Revelation, beginning with chapter six, a series of events takes place through seven seals, seven trumpets, and seven thunders. We will look at the last verse in chapter six which sets the stage for the sounding of the trumpets.

Revelation 6

17. for the great day of his wrath is come, and who shall be able to stand before him.

It is necessary to interpret many of the Scriptures of the Old Testament in the light of the New Testament of our Lord Jesus. However, the keys to being able to interpret the significance of the signs and symbols of the book of The Revelation of Jesus Christ are found in the Old Testament. In the Old Testament, the trumpet was made from a ram's horn and was called a shofar, which was blown to alert the people to danger and announce that there was shelter and protection in God. It was used in battles as an alarm and as a signal and is a symbol of the voice of God.

The ram is a symbol of the Lord Jesus, and the horn is associated with power. In the Old Testament battle of Jericho, the Israelites marched once around the city, blowing a shofar each day for six days. But on the seventh day, they blew seven trumpets and marched around the city seven times. The people were not allowed to shout during the first six days. On the seventh day, after blowing seven trumpets and marching around the city seven times, the trumpets sounded the jubilee. The people shouted and the walls of Jericho fell down flat. This was the end of the defenses of Jericho.

Only one woman and her family were saved out of the city of Jericho because they had received and protected the two spies that Joshua sent, and they had placed a sign of protection (a line of scarlet thread) in the window. Afterwards, this same woman married one of the spies that she had protected and became part of the line of the generations of Christ. Even though she was not an Israelite, she was a Gentile among the pagans of the land of Canaan (Scripture records that she was a harlot) and she received the people of God and the Lord received her.

A woman can symbolize an entire congregation or people. God describes Israel as a woman. In the New Testament, the bride of Christ is the congregation of believers. When much of Israel rejected the gospel, Scripture says that God cut off the unbelieving, disobedient branches of the good olive tree and grafted in wild branches of believing Gentiles just as Rahab, the harlot of Jericho, was grafted into Israel (Romans 11:17-24).

With Israel and the church, Christ is not doing two different things. *For through him we both have access by one Spirit unto the Father* (Ephesians 2:11-22). The goal of the Lord in all the long process of the gospel is that there might be more sons of God that may reign with Him who may receive responsibility, power, and authority with Him. The Lord wants these sons to receive the inheritance. The servants in the house do not receive the inheritance; the sons receive the inheritance. The Lord desires that we become sons, and in order to be the sons of God, we must allow Him to discipline us as sons. In this context the word *sons* is not referring exclusively to the masculine gender because in Christ there is no male nor female (Galatians 3:28).

The message of the seventh trumpet will sound along with the previous six, for all the trumpets will sound on the last day. What happened at Jericho was only a practice session, an example and a figure of what the Lord is doing in the end times. The Lord has been sounding a message throughout the entire age of the church. The first apostles sounded the first trumpet, and then after two or three hundred years the Lord raised up other ministries to sound other messages that were slightly different for another audience with different problems. As we have come through the Reformation, the Great Awakening, and the restoration of gifts and ministry of the Spirit, each successive trumpet has sounded.

Now we are entering the seventh millennium. This is the seventh prophetic day. Scripture says that one day is as a thousand years, and a thousand years are as a day before the Lord (Psalm 90:4; 2 Peter 3:8). Now we are at the moment when the Lord will sound the seventh trumpet. When this happens, all the wisdom and counsel of God will focus on this instant in time. All seven trumpets will sound and break the system of this world, and the only thing that will be saved out of it will be a people represented by the harlot woman, Rahab, who did receive the people that God sent.

Christian groups organized by men have had their problems and deviations similar to Rahab, the harlot of Jericho. But even in the times of utmost apostasy, there have always been those who have been willing to receive the true messengers of the Lord. The Lord even told the people of Israel, the Jews, that they would not see Him again until they said, *Blessed is he that comes in the name of the Lord* (Matthew 23:39; Luke 13:35).

The Lord Jesus came in the name of His Father and was not received. But when the Jewish people receive those sent by the Lord, a tremendous restoration and restitution of the glory that should have descended upon them two thousand years ago will occur. The apostle Paul wrote that when this happens it will be nothing less than *life from the dead* (Romans 11:15).

This is not about the restitution of rites and traditions. What the Lord desires for the Jewish people, for the people of Israel and for us, is life from the dead, resurrection life. This is the life of the Lord Jesus to enable us to live the message so we might flow in the fullness of the power of God in a way that we have not had access to before.

Revelation 9 (last verse)

21. *And they did not repent of their murders nor of their witchcraft nor of their fornication nor of their thefts.*

Revelation 10

1. *And I saw another mighty angel come down from heaven, clothed with a cloud; and a rainbow was upon his head, and his face was as the sun, and his feet as pillars of fire:*

This is the same description of the glorified Lord Jesus recorded in Revelation chapter 1. In this context of the past six thousand years of recorded human history in the Bible, the trumpets have been sounding. God has been sending prophets, apostles, leaders, and other ministries, but the vast majority of these have been rejected.

The system of this world has not repented. This is where we have arrived after six thousand years. With the sound of the six trumpets, the message of God has been going forth. A small remnant has received it, but general repentance has not taken place. The world continues to go from bad to worse with murders, witchcraft, fornication, and thefts. Colombia is no exception, but this is going on all over the place.

Even in places that used to be so peaceful, such as my native Minnesota in the United States, reports abound of greatly increased murder, shootouts on the streets and such, that a few decades ago were not the case. We are entering a stage of lawlessness and depravity in the entire world. These problems will intensify, but the solution from the Lord is His Word.

Before these trumpets, there was a stage of seven messages to the seven churches. Then seven seals had to be opened, which is the work of the Holy Spirit preparing hearts to receive the message. Then come the seven trumpets, and when the seventh trumpet is about to sound,

> *We are entering a stage of lawlessness and depravity in the entire world.*

there are seven thunders. The seven thunders are not written down because John was ordered not to do so. The seven thunders are a message of God for the end time; they go together with the seventh trumpet.

There are other groups of seven in the book of Revelation. The literal name of God, *I AM*, is announced seven times throughout the book (Revelation 1:8, 11, 17; 2:23; 21:6; 22:13, 16). He is the only one who exists for all eternity, and if we wish to have an eternal existence, it must be in Him. But we cannot do this on our own apart from Him.

The Lord Jesus began His ministry with seven beatitudes, and seven beatitudes are scattered throughout the book of Revelation, which correspond to the seven thunders and are related to the seventh trumpet. All of this is in the gospel, the gospel with depth. This will all come forth with force and anointing in the fullness and power of God. This will not be with just a measure of the Spirit of God, but with all the fullness of the power of the Spirit of God. This is what we may expect in this final time. On the one hand, the murders, witchcraft, fornication, and thefts continue. But on the other hand, the Spirit of God will intensify the message coming from the mouths of the true preachers of the Lord and of all the people of God. All of God's people will live and breathe God's truth.

Some will be sealed at a certain stage; God's judgments will not harm those who are sealed (Revelation 7:3). On the other hand, some will receive the mark of the beast on their hand or on their forehead (Revelation 13:16). We know that the enemy has plans, but in our natural state, a beast exists inside each and every one of us. We have a wild nature that does not want to submit to the Lord but that wants to dominate and control. The Word of God is available to cut this control of the flesh and penetrate into the most intimate depths of our heart.

Many believe that the mark of 666 could be a credit card or a microchip that will be implanted in the hands or foreheads of the people. This is not what I fear; what we really need to fear is doing things according to the beast nature that all of us are born with. The 666 is a manner of thinking and acting that marks the person who is not converted. It is possible that there may be an overt sign in the end times, but over the course of history since this was written almost two thousand years ago, this mark has existed. This manner of acting and thinking has existed all this time. These are not new things, but with time they have begun to intensify. The Lord Jesus summed up the truth that had already been taught in a new light.

John 10

8. *All that ever came before me are thieves and robbers, but the sheep did not hear them.*

Why? Because all who came before have stolen the glory of God. Even Moses, who was the meekest man on the face of the earth, had a moment of anger and took the glory of God for himself and in that moment disqualified himself from inheriting the Promised Land (Numbers 20:8-12). The only one who can enter the fullness of the inheritance is the Lord Jesus. If we are to enter into this, we must do it in Him. We must renounce that which is our own so that our life may be hid in the life of the Lord Jesus.

The number seven is framed into many Scripture passages. In the gospel according to Matthew, the Lord begins His message with seven beatitudes in the following manner:

Matthew 5

3. Blessed are the poor in spirit, for theirs is the kingdom of the heavens.

This means that whoever will not allow God to strip them of their pride and arrogance cannot enter the kingdom of God. Whoever desires to continue in command, being their own god, cannot enter the kingdom of the heavens because only the poor in spirit have God as their King.

In the same manner, the Lord's Prayer also has seven phrases, which line up with the seven beatitudes of Jesus, which line up with the seven thunders of the book of Revelation, which line up with the seven beatitudes of Revelation, which line up with the seven *I AM*s of Revelation. The message is not all that complicated.

For example, the first beatitude of Jesus is *Blessed are the poor in spirit, for theirs is the kingdom of the heavens.* Then in the Lord's Prayer it says, *Our Father who art in the heavens, Hallowed be thy name.* His name (nature) must be exalted above ours. We must submit to Him and seek His nature instead of our own. This is the entrance requirement.

Here is the first beatitude of Revelation:

Revelation 1

3. *Blessed is he that reads and those that hear the words of this prophecy and keep those things which are written therein, for the time is at hand.*

The poor in spirit are those who will enter the kingdom of God. We must leave our pride and arrogance behind if we are to enter the kingdom of the heavens. Every human being is born with the tendency toward pride, arrogance, and the desire to be the center of everything. Every small child wants to be the center of attention. God creates us innocent, according to the Scriptures (see Jeremiah 2:34, Ecclesiastes 7:29, 1 Timothy 4:4, Romans 9:11; compare Psalm 51:5 with the Jubilee Bible and track the word *innocent* through the Jubilee Bible), but as soon as we exercise our will, we begin to impose it on others and upon God. This is where we all get into trouble. This is where we need treatment. If not taken care of, we cannot enter the kingdom of God (remember Genesis 6:5; 8:21).

> ...*as soon as we exercise our will, we begin to impose it on others and upon God.*

What does it mean to enter the kingdom of God? It means being governed by God instead of having our own government. This key point recurs all through the Bible. It is the central point of the entire message, and if this is not dealt with, we cannot enter.

Here is the first *I AM* in Revelation:

8. *I AM the Alpha and the Omega, beginning and end, saith the Lord, who is and who was and who is to come, the Almighty.*

Scripture says *that he who has begun a good work in you will perfect it until the day of Jesus Christ* (Philippians 1:6). The Lord is the one who begins the work in us and who can also finish it, but we must yield to the Spirit of God. If we are not willing to yield, we can quench the Holy Spirit.

The second beatitude:

Matthew 5

4. *Blessed are those that mourn, for they shall be comforted.*

This is the word used to mourn a dead person, and the word *comforted* is from the same root as used by the apostle John when he wrote that we will be sent the Comforter, which is the Holy Spirit (John 14:26). Without the Comforter, without the Holy Spirit, no change can take place in our life and we will not be able to fulfill what God requires of us.

The third beatitude:

5. *Blessed are the meek, for they shall inherit the earth.*

Whoever has not received the Comforter cannot be meek (obey only the Master) and, therefore, will not be able to inherit the earth.

The fourth beatitude:

6. *Blessed are those who hunger and thirst for righteousness, for they shall be satisfied.*

The person who has not had a change of appetites can never be satisfied. Those who hunger and thirst after their own desires to be the center of everything, and have the mark of the beast with the way of acting and thinking of the old man, can never be satisfied. They can never be at peace. Only when the Lord governs our life and sends us the Comforter can we be comforted, filled, and satisfied. Then we will be able to receive the inheritance of the sons of God.

The fourth beatitude is the balancing point. The number four in Scripture refers to the heavens. On the fourth day of creation, the Lord created the heavenly bodies, such as the sun, moon, and stars (Genesis 1:14-19). The number four also has to do with the love of God. We are not born with this; it comes with the second birth. In order for the love of God to flow through us, we must have a change in appetite. The love of God is very different from the love of man. Man's love always requires something in return. The love of God does not.

The phrase in the Lord's Prayer that matches the fourth beatitude is *Give us this day our daily bread*.

Here is the fourth beatitude in Revelation:

Revelation 19

9. *And he said unto me, Write, Blessed are those who are called unto the marriage supper of the Lamb. And he said unto me, These are the true words of God.*

The marriage supper of the Lamb is a banquet of the Word of God that truly comes forth from Him and is not mixed up with doctrines of men. The person who has had a change of appetite no longer desires doctrines cooked up and leavened by man. All of the churches are full of truths of God mixed up with the leaven of man. We need to return to a clean, pure Word. So there is a need for vessels, for messengers, for clean people who can be bearers of this Word. Otherwise, the Word may not go forth clean.

But God promises the invited guests to this wedding supper the food will be clean. Why? Because the Father will marry His Son to a clean people, a people represented by a woman (bride) without spot or wrinkle or any such thing (Ephesians 5:27). She cannot be in the midst of all this leaven (1 Corinthians 5:6-8). This is why none of the religious groups organized by man qualify. God is choosing a remnant that is leaving many different places to come and participate in something that is clean. When the Lord calls and when the person responds to the voice of the Lord, He promises that He can finish the work.

If lightning represents the presence and coming of the Lord, then thunder represents the direct voice of God (Matthew 24:7; Luke 17:24; John 12:24-30). This is what the children of Israel rejected at Mount Sinai. They thought they would die if they listened to God's voice any longer. And yes, prolonged exposure to the voice and presence of God will definitely put an end to the old nature, to the old man that we inherited from Adam. This, however, is the requirement for entering into the inheritance of the new man in Christ.

We must not write off those who have remained behind, those who have not understood the garbled, mixed-up message coming from many churches filled with those who do not practice what they preach. The person who is blind and cannot see certain things is limited. We can spend all day explaining colors to a blind man or a symphony to someone who is deaf. They will never understand unless God opens their eyes and their ears. This is why the Lord says, *He who has ears to hear, let him hear* (Matthew 13:9).

The fourth reference in Revelation to *I AM* is set in a very intense context within the letter to the angel of the church in Thyatira:

Revelation 2

20. *Notwithstanding I have a few things against thee because thou sufferest that woman Jezebel (who calls her-*

self a prophetess) to teach and to seduce my servants to commit fornication, and to eat things sacrificed to idols.

21. *And I have given her time to repent of her fornication, and she repented not.*

22. *Behold, I will cast her into a bed and those that commit adultery with her into great tribulation unless they repent of their deeds.*

23. *And I will kill her children with death, and all the congregations shall know that I AM he that searches the kidneys and hearts, and I will give unto each one of you according to your works.*

I AM is the same as the sacred, unpronounceable name of God written as YHWH in the Old Testament which the Jews pronounced as Adoni or Lord when they read the sacred text. For the Jews, this name could only be pronounced by God Himself or by someone under the direct inspiration of the Spirit of God, such as Moses or David, when they wrote portions of the sacred text.

Jezebel symbolizes a false church that gives out unclean, contaminated spiritual food and who produces bastard children who are spiritual sons of unclean spirits. And this is all happening within the church until the direct presence of God appears and puts an end to it.

This judgment that comes when the Lord searches *the kidneys and hearts* refers to the appetites that we have and what we have been eating. The state of our heart determines our desires or appetites, and our kidneys are the purification system for the blood that our heart pumps. If we have an appetite for good things, if we are eating good, clean, things, and if we are under discipline as true sons of God, then we will be doing good things, His things.

It is very interesting to see that in the book of Revelation there are fourteen chapters between the first and the second beatitude, and many things happen here. Remember that the first beatitude relates to surrendering or being stripped of our pride so that God can reign in our lives. If we must place our pride and arrogance on the altar, something must die. This is the death of our own way of doing things.

In the second beatitude, *Blessed are those that mourn,* is the word meaning "to mourn a dead person," *for they shall be comforted.* If the old-nature part of us is not identified with the death of Jesus, there will be no Comforter. God will not come to comfort our bad attitude and the arrogance that we received from Adam. The Holy Spirit comes to comfort the new thing that God is planting in us.

> *God will not come to comfort our bad attitude and the arrogance that we received from Adam.*

The book of Revelation includes seven messages to seven churches. Some churches were doing fine in one area and not in another. One church was doing incredible work, except that they had left their first love. Now the love of God was not flowing through them as before. He told them, *Remember, therefore, from where thou art fallen and repent and do the first works, or else I will come unto thee quickly and will remove thy lampstand out of its place, except thou repent* (Revelation 2:5). He threatened to remove the light of His presence from among them unless this situation was rectified.

We see here terrible judgment directed toward the natural man, but incredible blessing for the new man in Christ. After this comes the opening of the seals as the Lamb that is worthy (Jesus) opens the seals of God's covenant and applies them to our hearts by the power of the Holy Spirit. This ends with an open heaven where all those who dwell on the land (Israel and the church) or in the sea (world) seek to run and hide and cover themselves. God's true sons are then sealed so that none of the judgments of God upon the old creation can harm them, and the seventh seal is opened.

The sealed of God who are clean do not have to fear this day. It is a day of great authority, which sets the stage for the seven trumpets of God to begin to sound. On an earlier day, when Jesus was being baptized in the Jordan, the Father spoke from heaven and said, *This is my beloved Son, in whom I am well pleased* (Matthew 3:17; Mark 1:11; Luke 3:22). Now there are many sons dressed in white robes unto whom the heavens are open (Revelation 7:13-17).

With an open heaven, Jesus clearly had no communication problems with His Father. He did not even have to pray like we do. He did so to give an example to His disciples and so we could learn certain things. But He was so tuned in to the heart of the Father that when He did something, it was the work of the Father flowing through Him. For He could say, *I and my Father are one.* He said that He wants us to be one with Him just as He and the Father are one (John 17:21). He desires to be one with us, so He might share the same clarity (or glory) that the Father bestowed on Him with us. This is the message of the seventh trumpet of the Revelation of Jesus Christ.

To go from the poor in spirit to those who receive the Comforter without measure takes fourteen chapters in the book of Revelation. The message to the churches and the work of the Holy Spirit cutting, working, and applying these truths to the heart establishes a clean people and an open heaven. Then the message of God comes forth as forceful trumpet blasts with power to change and to convert and to judge.

Here is the second beatitude of Revelation:

Revelation 14

12. *Here is the patience of the saints; here are those that keep the commandments of God and the faith **of** Jesus.*

13. *And I heard a voice from heaven saying unto me, Write, Blessed are the dead who die in the Lord from now on; Yea, saith the Spirit, that they may rest from their labours, and their works do follow them* (emphasis added).

These are the people who die to their own works but their works follow them (while they rest). What works? The works of God done in and through them. These are those who keep the commandments of God and the faith **of** Jesus. Modern translations have changed this to faith **in** Jesus. Many verses in Scripture encourage us to place our faith and trust in Jesus, but this and other verses speak of us being able to appropriate (keep) the faith of Jesus which must work in and through us. Otherwise, we will never be able to keep the commandments of God. This is the key to having the second and third line of the Lord's Prayer become a reality: *Thy kingdom come. Thy will be done in earth, as it is in heaven.*

The only way that we can keep the commandments of God here on earth is if the faith of Jesus resides in us. Abraham believed God (and was willing to sacrifice his dear son Isaac) and it was counted unto him as righteousness. Jesus believed God the Father and went to the cross, gave His life, broke the power of sin and death, and is now seated at the right hand of the Father with all power and authority to work unlimited victory in and through us! With the faith of Jesus, we will be able to do the same works that He did, which is the will of God the Father here on earth. If we understand this and the old dies and passes away, the inspired words of the apostle Paul will become reality: *behold, all things are made new* (2 Corinthians 5:17).

We shall be new creatures in a new creation, firstfruits unto God and to the Lamb, and the first of the firstfruits is Jesus Christ. When He resides in us, we are part of His body of many members (the body of Christ). He will bring us to maturity so we can also do what He did – keep the commandments of God and constantly do the will of the Father here on earth. Jesus did not do anything on His own; He always did the will of His Father. At the sounding of the seventh trumpet, we will see the fulfillment of so many promises. Until this time, the sound of the trumpets has not been clear, but they have sounded according to the whims and customs of man (see 1 Corinthians 14:8). The world continues to be rebellious with its murders, witchcraft, fornication, and thefts on its downhill slide from bad to worse. But God's plan with the seventh trumpet will radically change everything.

> *Jesus did not do anything on His own; He always did the will of His Father.*

Let us examine the seventh angel, which represents Christ (Jesus, the head, in the heavens and the feet of the body on earth), clothed in a cloud, which represents the nature of God.

Revelation 10

1. And I saw another mighty angel come down from heaven, clothed with a cloud; and a rainbow was upon his head, and his face was as the sun, and his feet as pillars of fire:

The rainbow of many colors upon his head indicates a fulfilled covenant with God. This means that the will of God is being done on earth as it is in heaven. Jesus, the head, is in the heavens reigning at the right hand of the Father with all power as King and High Priest and the only Mediator to effect all His cleanness, all His goodness, all His forgiveness, and all His power in and through us. Those of us who are alive and remain here on the earth are part of His feet, and He will join the entire body together. Remember that the factor that opens the heavens and brings everything together in Christ is called holocaust. When we become a clean and living sacrifice before the Lord, the heavens open so that God can work in and through us. This word means "to ascend" (gain access into the heavenly realm).

> 2. *And he had in his hand a little open book, and he set his right foot upon the sea and his left foot upon the land.*

The sea is symbolic of the nations, while the land is symbolic of the people of God under law. When the Lord brings forth this ministry, He will have His right foot upon the sea of unconverted humanity and His left foot upon the church and Israel. This message is going to go everywhere. It will hit the people of God even in the midst of all their leaven, and it will hit those who do not even name the name of God.

This message will go forth with the same force everywhere because it is a message that will not only be proclaimed but it will be lived. John had to eat the scroll. This represents a people like John who have eaten this message – a people who have been to the wedding feast and have eaten this Word until it has become part of their being. This is not a people who have to prepare sermons or messages. This is a people who together are the message. Isaiah prophesied:

> *Behold, I and the children whom the LORD has given me are for signs and for wonders in Israel from the LORD of the hosts, who dwells in Mount Zion*
> (Isaiah 8:18).

The Lord will have a people who will be a prophetic and an apostolic statement of who He is, because they are His body here on the earth. The two feet are the representation of this.

> 3. *And cried out with a loud voice as when a lion roars; and when he had cried out, seven thunders uttered their voices.*

This is a message that will enter with overwhelming force. Jesus is the lion of the tribe of Judah and thunder is linked to the direct voice of God the Father (see Revelation 5:5, Psalm 77:18, John 12:29).

> 4. *And when the seven thunders had uttered their voices,*

The seven thunders are the fulfillment of the beatitudes announced by our Lord Jesus, which are fulfilled in the book of Revelation, but which work through a people who are the body of Christ here on the earth who are one with Jesus and with the Father (see John 17). This is a message that is not only preached, but must be lived out so that those seven thunders will speak. Where there is thunder, there must also be lightning. Lightning is the symbol of the direct presence of God, which is what changes and converts.

Until now, much of the church has had seminaries, has trained leaders, has summoned the people to convocations, and has done many other things *having the appearance of godliness, but denying the power thereof* (2 Timothy 3:5). Formation is not enough; a transformation is required, and this only happens with the presence of God. The presence of God transforms. The first six trumpets did not produce overwhelming repentance in the church or in the world, because the lightning of the force of the direct presence of God in fullness was not there. This transforming presence was reserved for the time of the second coming of Christ.

The second coming of Christ has many stages just as His first coming did. The first coming of Christ had appearances of angels such as Gabriel. The Holy Spirit overshadowed Mary, and that which was conceived in her was the coming of God in her. The child was born and the heavenly choirs appeared to shepherds who were watching their flocks by night. The baby was presented in the temple and only Simeon and Anna were there. The wise men saw the child. The boy appeared in the temple and the majority of the priests did not know what they really had before them. The Son of God was baptized in the Jordan, the heavens were opened, and the Father spoke (a few people understood, but most did not). The glory of God was revealed by the ministry, death, resurrection, and ascension of Jesus Christ. The Spirit was poured out on believers at Pentecost. The world was turned upside down (Acts 17:6).

Even greater things will happen now. There will be a people who will receive a special presence inside, like Mary, and become "pregnant" with the plans and purposes of God. There will be shepherds (pastors) watching their "flocks" by night, and they will receive a special revelation that those who are "asleep" will know nothing about. Wise men will follow the light, but so will others who think they are wise but do not see anything until it is too late.

The fire of God has gone out on several occasions over the history of the people of Israel. The sacred fire of God had to be continually lit on the altar (Leviticus 6:12). It could not just be any fire. It had to be a fire lit by God and not by man. This fire went out many times in Israel and the same is true for the church. Only God can decide when and where to relight the fire of His presence. However, on the day of Pentecost when the fire of God came back, it was not at the altar of the temple; rather, the Lord lit the people on fire. The Holy Spirit fell on the people, and there were tongues of fire resting on each one of them (Acts 2). The Lord said that He would no longer dwell in temples made of stone by the hands of man. The people of God would be His temple (1 Corinthians 3:16, 17). The stone that the builders rejected is the Lord Jesus, and He is the one who baptizes in the Holy Spirit and fire. He is still available to light His fire in each and every one of us.

This is the part that we have been going over and over between the first and second beatitude. We must recognize our spiritual need, open our lives to the Lord, and conduct a funeral over the death of all that needs to die in us so the Comforter and the fire of God can be lit in us. There is no other way to become meek to do the will of God and hunger and thirst for righteousness.

> 5. *And the angel whom I saw standing upon the sea and upon the land lifted up his hand to heaven*
>
> 6. *and swore by him that lives for ever and ever, who created the heaven and the things that are therein, and the earth, and the things that are therein, and the sea and the things which are therein, that there should be time no longer;*
>
> 7. *but in the day of the voice of the seventh angel when he shall begin to sound the trumpet, the mystery of God shall be finished, as he did evangelize unto his slaves the prophets.*

All of the prophets have announced the day that we are entering, when the mystery of God shall be no longer hidden and we may understand the purpose of God in us. This is the message of the seventh trumpet and the seven thunders.

The Lord created the heavenly hosts and the realm of heaven. The earth is the realm of Israel, and most of the church has opted for a covenant of law (they make up their own rules, regulations and doctrines). The sea is the realm of lost humanity (Gentile nations). Everything taking place in the heavenly spiritual realm seems to have an earthly counterpart. If we are truly born from above, the heavenly Jerusalem is the mother of us all. If our true citizenship is of heaven, we will have nothing to fear as future events of the day of the Lord unfold. *Therefore, rejoice, ye heavens, and ye that dwell in them. Woe to the inhabiters of the earth and of the sea!* (Revelation 12:12)

We are in the day when the voice of the seventh angel will begin to sound. Each one of these trumpets is the voice of God through a messenger (the word *angel* simply means "messenger" in Hebrew and can apply to the heavenly angelic host or to men and women of flesh and blood here on earth if God decides to use them). All of the trumpets will now sound together as we enter the seventh millennial day, known throughout the Scriptures as the day of the Lord. Immediately leading up to the seventh trumpet, the seven thunders of the direct voice of God will sound along with the lightning-clear revelation of Jesus Christ.

> *If our true citizenship is of heaven, we will have nothing to fear as future events of the day of the Lord unfold.*

Revelation 11

15. *And the seventh angel sounded the trumpet, and there were great voices in heaven, saying, The kingdoms of this world are reduced unto our Lord and to his Christ; and he shall reign for ever and ever.*

16. *And the twenty-four elders, who sat before God on their thrones, fell upon their faces and worshipped God,*

17. *saying, We give thee thanks, O Lord God Almighty, who art and wast, and art to come because thou hast taken to thee thy great power and hast reigned.*

18. *And the Gentiles were angry, and thy wrath is come, and the time of the dead, that they should be judged, and that thou should give the reward unto thy slaves the prophets and to the saints that fear thy name, to the small and to the great, and should destroy those who destroy the earth.*

19. *And the temple of God was opened in heaven, and the ark of his testament was seen in his temple: and there were lightnings and voices and thunderings and earthquakes and great hail.*

The kingdoms of this world shall fall, and the Lord shall reign forever and ever. We are His temple: Jesus Christ is *the ark of his testament,* and we are part of this if we belong to the true body of Christ.

The Comforter comes so that we may become meek, fulfill the will of God, and hunger and thirst for righteousness (which means being and doing what God desires). He comes so we may go to the wedding banquet, receive our daily bread directly from the Lord (*Man shall not live by bread alone, but by every word that proceeds out of the mouth of God*), and have intimate communion with God with an open heaven as sons of God. He comes so creation might be redeemed and there may be new heavens and a new earth (Romans 8, Isaiah 66).

CHAPTER 7

Participating in the Plan of Redemption

—————————⚓—————————

So what does the Lord require of us so that we might participate in His plan of redemption?

Micah 6

8. *He has declared unto thee, O man, what is good and what the LORD requires of thee: only to do right judgment, and to love mercy, and to humble thyself to walk with thy God.*

The fifth beatitude, *Blessed are the merciful, for they shall obtain mercy.* The fifth line from the Lord's Prayer says, *And set us free from our debts, as we set free our debtors.* To *set free* is slightly different than to *forgive.* It has been translated forgive, but the Bibles of the early Reformation speak of everyone being set free. Jesus told us that we should be willing to forgive *unto seventy times seven* (Matthew 18:22). But what if our brother has not come to ask for forgiveness? The Lord wants us to unilaterally let go of the matter so we may all be set free and so that the evil that has been done to us will not continue to eat away at us. We can then let go and trust in the justice of God, for the Lord says, *Vengeance [is] mine* (Deuteronomy 32:35).

Romans 12

17. Not repaying anyone evil for evil; procuring that which is good not only in the sight of God, but even in the sight of all men.

18. If it can be done, as much as is possible on your part, live in peace with all men.

19. Not defending yourselves, dearly beloved; but rather give place unto the wrath of God, for it is written, Vengeance is mine, I will repay, saith the Lord.

20. Therefore, if thine enemy hungers, feed him; if he thirsts, give him drink; for in so doing thou shalt heap coals of fire on his head.

21. Do not be overcome by evil, but overcome evil with good.

Some may think that to *heap coals of fire on his head* is to destroy our enemy, but in ancient times they did not have matches. If the fire went out in someone's home, they would have to go over to the neighbor's and bring back some coals of fire in a clay vessel that they would carry on their head. If the fire of the love of God has gone out in our neighbor, we may be able to help them if we are willing to overcome evil with good.

> *Our human love is always requiring something in return; the love of God is not.*

This is the motive for the new commandment that the Lord gave us concerning the law of love. Our human love is always requiring something in return; the love of God is not. Here centers the message of the merciful. The Lord taught me about this as I flew airplanes in the jungle. He put it in my heart to be merciful and help anyone in need, take them to the hospital, or whatever they needed even if they had no money. Many people apparently took advantage of me, but the Lord kept me safe and I never had an accident. I was able to fly thousands of hours. Most of my pilot friends killed themselves or were crippled in air accidents. Without being the best pilot, I never had any of these problems. Others had much better training and equipment, but the Lord put His hand on me and taught me the truth about right judgment, mercy, and a humble walk with God (Matthew 18:21-35).

The fifth beatitude in Revelation:

Revelation 20

4. *and they shall live and reign with Christ the thousand years.*

5. *But the rest of the dead did not live again until the thousand years were finished. This is the first resurrection.*

6. *Blessed and holy is he that has part in the first resurrection; on such the second death has no authority, but they shall be priests of God and of the Christ and shall reign with him a thousand years.*

So what is necessary in order to qualify for this promise? Be merciful. Allow the love and the mercy of God to flow through us.

Look at the fifth *I AM* in Revelation.

Revelation 21

5. *And he that was seated upon the throne said, Behold, I make all things new. And he said unto me, Write: for these words are faithful and true.*

6. *And he said unto me, It is done. I AM the Alpha and the Omega, the beginning and the end. I will give unto him that is thirsty of the fountain of the water of life freely.*

7. *He that overcomes shall inherit all things; and I will be his God, and he shall be my son.*

How can we receive the provision of the fountain of the water of life freely? We must have a thirst for it. We must hunger and thirst for righteousness. If we have been transformed by the power and presence of God, He will cause rivers of water to flow from our innermost being which will touch others with His truth, His mercy, and His grace. Those who seek selfish, personal benefit from the blessings of God will be disqualified from the first resurrection and will not participate in the one thousand years of the government of God upon the earth; they will wake up just in time for the final judgment which could go one way or the other for them.

8. *But the fearful and unbelieving and the abominable and murderers and fornicators and sorcerers and idolaters and all liars shall have their part in the lake of fire which burns with fire and brimstone, which is the second death.*

The sixth beatitude:

Matthew 5

8. *Blessed are the pure in heart, for they shall see God.*

The sixth line in the Lord's Prayer is *And lead us not into temptation, but deliver us from evil.* If we have a pure heart, temptation will have no hold on us. What contaminates a person is not what is outside in the corrupt world we live in, but what is inside. If the heart is not clean, everything that flows out of that person will be contaminated. Some think that they would be fine if they could just find a little enclave away from the world where there were no drugs, no vice, no temptations, and that this would solve their problem. This is not true. It will do no good to seek "clean" surroundings. We must have a clean heart! If the Lord cleanses us from within, nothing on the outside will be able to affect us. We can be in the most terrible spot in the world, and nothing will happen to us because we will flow in the purity of God.

Jesus faced these same situations. He was near a funeral, and when He touched the dead body, Jesus did not become unclean; instead, the dead man came back to life (Luke 7:11-14).

The sixth beatitude of Revelation:

Revelation 22

7. Behold, I come quickly; blessed is he that keeps the words of the prophecy of this book.

Who may be able to keep the words of the prophecy of this book? The pure in heart. Here is the sixth *I AM* of Revelation:

13. I AM the Alpha and the Omega, beginning and end, the first and the last.

He is the one who initiates the work. He is the one who finishes the work. Our role in all of this is to be docile in His hands, to be soft clay in the hands of the Potter so He may form us into what He had in mind from the beginning.

The seventh beatitude:

Matthew 5

9. Blessed are the peacemakers, for they shall be called the sons of God.

The last line in the Lord's Prayer is *for thine is the kingdom and the power and the glory forever. Amen* (Matthew 6:13).

The sons of God who will receive the inheritance will not take this for themselves because they know it all belongs to Him. They are like the twenty-four elders who throw their crowns at His feet before the throne saying, *Thou art worthy, O Lord, to receive glory and honor and virtue* (Revelation 4:11). This is a government where the Lord will delegate responsibility to those who will not return to the pride and arrogance that all fallen humans have had and instead have demonstrated that they will continue to be meek and humble before the throne of God. They will reign with Christ and govern the earth.

The seventh beatitude in Revelation:

Revelation 22

14. *Blessed are those who do his commandments that their power and authority might be in the tree of life and they may enter in through the gates into the city.*

The tree of life is what Adam and Eve lost. They chose the tree of the knowledge of good and of evil. They chose to be their own god and to decide for themselves what was good and what was evil. Among the people of God (referring to the Jews and to the church), we have let God decide what is evil, while much of the time we continue to decide what is good. Our failure to completely yield the knowledge of good and of evil back to God has cost us our access back to the tree of life.

The Lord placed cherubim with a flaming sword to keep the way of the tree of life (Genesis 3:24). These cherubim with the flaming sword were embroidered on the veil between the Holy Place and the Holy of Holies, symbolizing that no one could get back into the presence of God without passing through the judgment of the sword of the Lord (Exodus 36:35). The old man must die so we can enter as the new man in Christ. The Lord Jesus has already entered in and has broken the veil from top to bottom, and He is now in heavenly places with all power and glory. But here on earth we continue to sew up the veil because we do not want to die to our own way. But there will be a people who will enter through the door. What is the door? He is the door. Whoever enters by the door enters into Him. Whoever enters into Him cannot continue in their own will. He is the root and offspring of David.

Revelation 3

7. And to the angel of the congregation in Philadelphia write: These things, saith he that is Holy and True, he who has the key of David, who opens and no one shuts and shuts, and no one opens;

The key of David is mentioned in only two Scriptures: one in each Testament (Isaiah 22:22; Revelation 3:7). The key of David is not a magic formula. The path to victory is to return the knowledge of good and evil to the Lord. If we think something is wonderful, and

If we think something is wonderful, and He wants to shut the door, so be it.

He wants to shut the door, so be it. If we only walk through the doors that He opens, no one will be able to shut them. The brethren overcame by the blood of the Lamb and by the truth of their testimony and because they loved not their lives unto death (Revelation 12:11).

Here is the seventh and last *I AM.*

Revelation 22

16. I, Jesus, have sent my angel to testify unto you these things in the congregations. I AM the root and the offspring of David and the bright and morning star.

The six-pointed star that many Jews try to represent with two triangles likely comes from pagan roots dating back to the apostasy of Solomon. But even if it is a representation of the star of David, there is a problem, for we have been ordered not to *make unto thee any graven image or any likeness of anything that is in heaven above or that is in the earth beneath nor that is in the water under the earth* (Exodus 20:4). The star of David, the morning star, is Jesus, and we may not make images of Jesus.

For this reason, a better symbol of Israel is the menorah, the lampstand with seven flames of fire, which the Lord uses in Revelation to represent the presence and fire of God in each of the seven churches. The six-pointed star is not found in the book of Revelation. Many use it in good faith, as people in other churches use statues of a given person or icons, but they present the same problem. The Lord does not want us to worship something made with our own hands; He wants us to only worship Him. We are to worship in spirit and in truth.

> 17. *And the Spirit and the bride say, Come. And let Him that hears say, Come. And let him that is thirsty come; and whosoever will, let him take of the water of life freely.*

The Lord is going to open the way for the flow of the water of the Spirit of God for whoever is thirsty, for whosoever will come. For the Spirit and the bride are saying the same thing; they bear the same witness. The bride is not saying one thing and the Spirit another. The Lord desires a clear message where the preaching by the inspiration of the Spirit of God is the same as what the people of God are saying while living here on earth.

Regarding Revelation 11, much speculation has arisen as to exactly who the two witnesses are. Some say Moses and Enoch, others say Moses and Elijah, others say the Old and the New Testaments, and so on. The two witnesses that are depicted throughout the book of Revelation are him and her: the Spirit and the bride, a clean people of God here on the earth being in tune with the Spirit of God and bearing a clear witness. They overcome by the blood of the Lamb (by His life in them, Christ in you, the hope of glory), by the truth of their testimony, and because they loved not their lives unto death. The Lord can apply this as He sees fit. This is the representation of the angel with his head in heaven, clothed in a cloud (of the nature of God), and his two feet, one on the land and one on the sea as pillars of fire (lit with the fire of God).

The Lord showed me that in order not to be rudely awakened when He returns, it is necessary to stay in the fire of God. The fire of God is the correction and discipline of God for His sons whom He loves. To stay in the fire is to be willing to do whatever He desires, whenever He decides, and however He wishes His will to be accomplished. We must receive, embrace, and authorize the Spirit of God to apply those seven thunders so the lightning of the presence of God may remain lit and burning brightly within all of us. This is not about an individual ministry here or there. This is a vision of the body of Christ *fitly joined together and well tied together* coming forth in all the power and victory of God.

Revelation 11

15. *And the seventh angel sounded the trumpet, and there were great voices in the heaven, saying, The kingdoms of this world are reduced unto our Lord and to his Christ; and he shall reign for ever and ever.*

This does not say that He is going to take over the kingdoms of this world and manage them. The kingdoms of this world are reduced. The walls of Jericho fall down flat. Everything comes down, and the Lord reigns through a people He has called and chosen and who have been proven faithful. Only one woman, one family, one group of people was saved. A woman who was a harlot received the messengers of the Lord. She hung a scarlet thread in the window. The blood of the Lamb was applied. The blood of the Lord proclaims that we have entered into His death, and because of this, we are willing for Him to bring down anything that needs to die in our being. Scripture states that the life is in the blood (John 6:53). When His blood is applied to us in this manner, the Spirit of God is present and provides comfort. His life is present in us. His fire is lit in us. His faith comes forth in us. His victory is for us to live the message of the Word of God.

> 16. *And the twenty-four elders, who sat before God on their thrones, fell upon their faces and worshipped God,*

> 17. *saying, We give thee thanks, O Lord God Almighty, who art and wast, and art to come because thou hast taken to thee thy great power and hast reigned.*

> 18. *And the Gentiles were angry, and thy wrath is come, and the time of the dead, that they should be judged, and that thou should give the reward unto thy servants the prophets and to the saints and those that fear thy name, to the small and to the great, and should destroy those who destroy the earth.*

> 19. *And the temple of God was opened in heaven, and the ark of his testament was seen in his temple: and there were lightnings and voices and thunderings and earthquakes and great hail.*

The seventh trumpet will sound. Everything that can be shaken will be shaken so we might be given a kingdom that can never be shaken (Hebrews 12:25-29).

Let us pray

Heavenly Father, we ask for eyes to see and ears to hear, that we might enter as poor in spirit to be governed by Christ though the Holy Spirit, that we might receive the Comforter of your presence, and that your Spirit may flow through us to change us until we are able to be meek and do your will. We ask that we may have a change in appetites to hunger and thirst for righteousness. May we become merciful and flow in the rivers of water of life until we are pure in heart, washed by your Word which has circulated through us, and have become the sons of God ready to receive the inheritance – not to do our will but to do your will. We ask this in the name of our Lord Jesus. Amen.

About the Author

Russell Stendal was raised in the mission field in Colombia, South America. He became a missionary jungle pilot at age nineteen. Almost ten years later, in 1983, he was kidnapped by Marxist rebels and held hostage for five months. His book, *Rescue the Captors*, relates his experience, including how God worked in the hearts of the rebels.

Russell has written many other books, produced videos, and edited two Bible translations, the Spanish Reina-Valera 2000 and the Jubilee Bible in English.

Russell heads up the work of Colombia Para Cristo, which operates twelve radio stations involving more than one hundred staff and coworkers and covering much of Latin America with the gospel. A thriving underground church has developed in remote jungle areas of Colombia. New high-gain antennas are now beaming the gospel message deep into areas of increasing crisis across the borders of Venezuela, Ecuador, Peru, and Brazil, as well as throughout Colombia.

More books by Russell Stendal:

Please review this book on Amazon:

Watch the La Montana trailer, a film based on a true Stendal event: